Protecting Children
from Exploitation
and Trafficking:
Using the Positive Deviance Approach
in Uganda and Indonesia

Protecting Children from Exploitation and Trafficking:

Using the Positive Deviance Approach

in Uganda and Indonesia

Arvind Singhal
and
Lucia Dura

Save the Children®

in collaboration with

Department of Communication
The University of Texas at El Paso

Front cover photo (credit - Lucia Dura and Arvind Singhal): Mother
and child in Pader District in Northern Uganda
Back cover photo (credit - Lucia Dura and Arvind Singhal): Young
girls in East Java, Indonesia with Save the Children Fieldworkers

Front and back cover design: Sara E. Sanchez
Content formatting: Sara E. Sanchez

ISBN: 978-0-615-31141-8

This monograph is dedicated to

Jerry Sternin

1938-2008

our friend and colleague, who inspired the use of the positive deviance approach to child protection in Indonesia and Uganda, saving and improving the lives of countless children. Jerry Sternin was a dedicated member of the Save the Children staff for 16 years.

Acknowledgements

The Life after the LRA: Piloting Positive Deviance with Child Mothers and Vulnerable Girl Survivors in Northern Uganda program was funded by the Oak Foundation, and the Positive Deviance to Reduce Trafficking of Young Girls in East Java, Indonesia program was funded by the Oak Foundation during a pilot phase and later by the United States Department of Labor. Arvind Singhal and Lucia Dura were contracted by Save the Children to conduct the project assessments in Uganda and Indonesia and develop this monograph for submission to the Oak Foundation.

We thank the following individuals for their help and support in carrying out the present research project: Anastasia Anthopoulos of Oak Foundation; Lisa Laumann, Dan Rono, and Samoa Pereira of Save the Children USA. Ms. Anthopoulos, Ms. Laumann, and Mr. Rono provided detailed comments on previous versions of this monograph. Thanks are also due to several Save the Children staff in Uganda, including Peter Nkhonjera, Tom Cole, Bonita Birungi, Luc Vanhoorickx, and others; the positive deviance (PD) team in Pader, including Robert Omara, Paska Aber, Simon Lukone, Jimmy, Beatrice, Raymond, Jennifer, Betty, and Nathan; Save the Children staff in Indonesia, including Catherine Chen, Didid, Kirik, Nina, Ruly, Witri, and Budi. A special thanks to Jerry and Monique Sternin for their encouragement and feedback on previous versions of this monograph, as also to Randa Wilkinson, former Save the Children Indonesia Country Office's PD nutrition expert, who generously shared her insights.

Table of Contents

Executive Summary 1

Part 1: Purpose and Structure of the Monograph 13

Part 2: The Positive Deviance Approach to Social Change 16

Part 3: Methodology and Data Collection 23

Part 4: Life after the LRA: Piloting Positive Deviance with Child Mothers and Vulnerable Girl Survivors in Northern Uganda 32

Part 5: Positive Deviance to Reduce Trafficking of Young Girls in East Java, Indonesia 74

Part 6: Conclusions, Lessons and Recommendations for Using Positive Deviance for Child Protection 114

References 145

Executive Summary

The positive deviance (PD) approach is an assets-based approach to social and behavior change that identifies solutions to community problems within the community.[1] Its premise is that in every community there are individuals or families whose practices and behaviors enable them to find better solutions to problems than their neighbors who have access to the same resources. In this approach, facilitators work with people to identify a common problem, find the individuals or families who practice uncommon but effective behaviors—the "positive deviants"—that enable them to overcome the common problem and promote those behaviors in the community.

The usefulness of the PD approach in changing behavior has been well documented in the fields of health and nutrition, but not in the child protection field. This monograph contributes to the knowledge base about the use of the approach in child protection programming. It analyzes two projects funded by the Oak Foundation and implemented by Save the Children that used the approach to address child protection issues: a project in Uganda to reintegrate girls who had been abducted by the Lords Resistance Army (LRA) and girl mothers into their communities, and a project in Indonesia to reduce the incidence of girl trafficking.

---

1 See www.positivedeviance.org

The study sought to give insight related to community engagement in finding solutions to child protection problems, planning and implementing related actions, and accounting for unanticipated consequences in these projects. It also aimed to strengthen understanding of how the PD approach can connect to programming at scale and the human resource investment needed to use the approach effectively. The study used in-depth interviews with participants, participatory sketching and accompanying narrations, and an analysis of existing archival materials in both Uganda and Indonesia to generate data. The analysis synthesizes several lessons on the use of the approach to address child protection issues. The monograph also presents implications for scaling up pilot projects and the conditions under which the PD approach can be most effective.

Uganda

In 2007 and 2008, Save the Children implemented a pilot program using the positive deviance approach, *Life after the LRA: Piloting Positive Deviance with the Child Mothers and Vulnerable Girl Survivors in Northern Uganda*, to assist in the empowerment and reintegration of young mothers and vulnerable girls in the Pader District. The project targeted 500 young mothers and vulnerable girl survivors as well as 50 adult mentors who provided community-based guidance, monitoring and general psychosocial support. Of the 500 girls, some 40 percent were formerly abducted child mothers, 50 percent were vulnerable mothers having one or more early pregnancy, and 10 percent were young girls who served as heads of household, responsible for the care of one or more siblings.

Through a positive deviance inquiry (PDI), a team including peer educators, mentors, sub-county representatives and NGO staff facilitated a community process to identify positive deviant girls (called PD girls) and develop a list of their characteristic practices. Positive deviant girls then identified the coping mechanisms they believed helped them engage in these practices. Building on this knowledge, on-the-ground action included creating peer support networks, enabling counseling and mentoring, developing income generating skills and skills in group management and providing small grants.

The study identified several of the positive deviant practices that participants believed had made a big difference in their socioeconomic empowerment and significantly improved their quality of life, earning them respect within the larger community.

- **Work harder, smarter, and together.** PD girls put in extra effort to attend to their gardens after school. They were able to boost their

3

production using modern agricultural production techniques such as intercropping. They adopted practical and innovative business skills that enabled them to take advantage of their daily activities to generate income. The girls also pulled together to increase their efficiency and marketability and came together for recreation activity, which to a great extent improved their social cohesion and had therapeutic value.

- **Respect oneself and others.** Respect was a significant characteristic common among all the PD girls. The PD girls had mentors who played a role in cultivating this attribute. "The girls are very respectful. I see my mentor role as being one of a chameleon. I am aware of what they are doing. But I do not interfere. I keep a close watch from the sideline," said mentor Anna.

Display business acumen, save, invest and learn. With time, PD girls acquired and practiced business skills related to planning, budgeting, diversifying, prioritizing, saving and investing. A 16-year-old beneficiary described one example of diversification. "With the small money I received from Save the Children, I hired a sewing machine. Now I'm repairing and selling secondhand clothes. I have made some sales, and I have the money in my pocket. I have three sacks of maize saved from my garden, and I also have another garden in which I grow eggplant and other vegetables. I have hired a boy who helps sell in the market when I'm not there."

Cumulatively, respondents' sketches and narrations suggested that great strides have been made in the reintegration of former abductees, child mothers and vulnerable girls into the mainstream Acholi society, which itself is inching toward a semblance of stability and rebuilding after a violent civil conflict. The lives of these child mothers and vulnerable girls appeared to have been jump started by the project program. Key changes noted in the monograph include improvement in the girls' physical, material and psychological well-being as well as in their business success, role modeling and social integration.

Indonesia

In 2000, an estimated 30 to 40 percent of all commercial sex workers in Indonesia were under age 18, suggesting a high incidence of girl trafficking. To address this problem, Save the Children piloted an anti-trafficking program in partnership with the East Java Institution for Community Research and Development. The goal of the program, which ran from December

2002 to February 2005, was to reduce the number of girls trafficked into the sex industry through appropriate and sustainable grassroots antitrafficking initiatives. In 2004, Save the Children launched a scaled-up program to address girl trafficking with funding from the U.S. Department of Labor. Twenty-three of the 100 communities involved in this second project—those already identified as "sending" communities, meaning that trafficking was already occurring—employed the positive deviance approach. This study focused on two communities in East Java: Gadungsari village in Malang District, where the approach was piloted beginning in mid-2003, and Kedoyo village in Tulungagung District, where a PD approach was used starting in April 2007.

In Gadungsari, an initial workshop with village-level development workers to explain the process for using the positive deviance approach led to the identification of girl trafficking as a problem. A mapping exercise followed, which generated the information that 90 percent of 140 missing community members were young girls, showed local power relationships and clarified specific issues faced by vulnerable girls. The community decided to focus on understanding the behaviors of positive deviant families, and through the PD inquiry process identified several strategies and practices that helped families to reduce their girls' vulnerability to trafficking:

- Engage in a variety of income-generating activities and grow diverse crops;
- Help daughters to establish a small business;
- Discuss openly with children the risks of working in the entertainment industry and support exploring of alternatives;
- Emphasize the value of formal and nonformal education for daughters;
- Allow daughters to work outside the village after close investigation of the employer and the kind of work the daughter would do;
- Require daughters to report home regularly via letters and phone if they take employment outside the village.

Over five years, the positive deviance approach pilot experience in Gadungsari not only led to positive outcomes in terms of trafficking prevention, but also to the mainstreaming of the approach in other village development sectors. It led to increased communication between parents and children, and girls targeted by the program continued in school and earned a minimum secondary education. Positive deviant families (called PD families) had varied sources of income, which raised their standard of living and reduced the risk of girls being trafficked. The knowledge gained by PD families was also shared. The community set up a village watch committee that kept a close eye on girls who left the village. Many parents purchased mobile telephone credit vouchers for girls who worked outside so that girls could call them at any time.   PD was also mainstreamed in all Gadungsari development plans.

While the positive deviance pilot project in Kedoyo village was less integrated into the village's fabric of development programs than in Gadungsari, there was evidence of its effectiveness a year after the start of the project. Community members identified multiple positive deviant behaviors that they believed made them better able to secure brighter futures for their children: saving more, studying more, learning more, working more and pursuing new vocational skills. Community members reported that both girls and boys were inspired to see other young people engaged in both education and income-generating activities, and noted an increase in group meetings about local development and in the interaction of community members with government officials.

In both Gadungsari and Kedoyo, PD families emphasized the value of both formal and nonformal education for their daughters, supported their daughters in establishing a business venture, engaged in a variety of income-generating activities, consciously saved money and found ways to connect their needs and aspirations with existing state-supported or state-sponsored programs. The availability of vocational training contributed to expanded learning opportunities for the village, leading to more local employment opportunities as well as enhanced incomes and personal savings.

The experiences in Gadungsari and Kedoyo point to two crucial elements in consolidating and expanding PD: First, community ownership of the positive deviance inquiry, of the subsequent understanding of its findings, and of the development of an actionable plan and, second, early formation and maintenance of strong relationships with partner NGOs and government officials at the local and regional levels. The findings suggest that success and sustainability are more likely to be attained when these elements are present.

Key Attributes of the Positive Deviance Approach and Lessons Learned

This study identifies key attributes of the positive deviance approach: It finds solutions close at hand, it promotes and builds on community ownership, it opens lines of communication and builds trust, it then expands on that trust and the respect it fosters, and it does not require special resources. This study also notes some lessons learned from using the approach to address child protection issues:

- **The PD approach to child protection is effective but not formulaic.** The approach can

9

be effective in addressing child protection because it provides skills, tools, and processes that can be implemented immediately and sustained over a long period. It privileges local wisdom and resources. It does not offer specific formulas for particular issues, though: Solutions develop through the process of inquiry, analysis, action planning and solution implementation.

The PD approach works best with real and intractable problems. The approach works well when, (1) the solution to the problem is essentially a non-technical one dealing with adaptive behavioral issues, (2) the problem is pervasive and intractable and worth the risk of attempting a new approach, (3) positive deviants do exist in the community, and (4) the community leaders and skilled facilitators are willing to champion the effort, be willing to learn and have faith in the innate wisdom that lies within the community.

The PD approach protects and prevents. The approach interfaces well with core protection issues. It does so by allowing beneficiaries to fully participate in their own protection and, in so doing, empowering them to help protect and support their siblings, family members and peers.

- **Small inputs, big impact.** The impact of the approach is greater than the input because it is community owned and driven. Like other social change approaches, it can also engender unintended impacts; in Indonesia and Uganda, the core processes used laid the groundwork for addressing other social concerns including reproductive health, gender and child rights, HIV/AIDS and gender violence.

- **Takes time but produces results.** The PD approach is a time- and skill-intensive approach. It takes time and skill to mobilize the community to respond to the problem and to overcome resistance to addressing sensitive issues. While the approach does not offer quick fixes, it leads to sustainable solutions. Local leaders and community members who become proficient in the approach continue to use their skills to sustain and strengthen the project and to apply the approach in other spheres of development.

- **Does not package well in a tool box.** The process of the approach and the solutions found through it are culture-specific and hard to predict. The approach requires mentoring, letting go of control and allowing the process to run its course. This can be a challenge for project donors and project implementers who want a level of predictability of outputs and outcomes that the approach does not provide.

- **Redefines scalability.** The full PD approach (with workshops, community-level positive deviance inquiry, group data analysis, participatory action planning, and implementation of solutions) is not easily or quickly scalable to cover large populations. However, it can scale along existing social networks and through permanent local stakeholder partnerships. In addition, the outcomes of the process can lead to changes on a larger canvas, for example, through influencing policy.

Part 1
Purpose and Structure of the Monograph

This monograph analyzes two positive deviance projects focused on child protection issues in Uganda and Indonesia implemented by Save the Children. Positive deviance (PD) is an approach to social change that enables communities to discover the wisdom they already have and then to act on it.[2] Its premise is that, in every community, certain individuals with uncommon practices/behaviors are enabled to find better solutions to problems than their neighbors who have access to the same resources. The two positive deviance projects analyzed were:

1.   *Life after the LRA: Piloting Positive Deviance with the Child Mothers and Vulnerable Girl Survivors in Northern Uganda.* The purpose of this pilot project, implemented since March 2007, was to assist in the empowerment and reintegration process of young mothers and vulnerable girls in Northern Uganda's conflict-ridden Pader District using the positive deviance approach. The Oak Foundation provided funding.

2.   *Positive Deviance to Reduce Trafficking of Young Girls in East Java, Indonesia.* The purpose of this project was to utilize the positive

---

2 Prucia Buscell, "The Power of Positive Deviance", *Emerging* (2004): 8-20; Jerry Sternin and Robert Choo, "The Power of Positive Deviance" *Harvard Business Review* (2000): 14-15; Richard Tanner Pascale and Jerry Sternin, "Your company's secret change agents". *Harvard Business Review* (2005): 1-11.

deviance approach to reduce girl trafficking in certain rural communities in East Java Province of Indonesia. We focused on two sites within East Java, where the PD program was implemented at different points in time Village Gadungsari in District Malang where the PD project was piloted in 2003 with funding from the Oak Foundation, and Village Kedoyo in District Tulungagung, where PD was launched in April 2007 as part of the Enabling Communities to Combat Child Trafficking through Education (ENABLE) project, funded by the U.S. Department of Labor.

PD project beneficiaries, Uganda and Indonesia

Our investigation of these projects consisted of a careful analysis of the existing archival documentation on both projects, as well as primary data-collection activities in both Uganda and Indonesia. Our investigation allowed us to synthesize the lessons learned about the use of the positive deviance approach for child protection programming, raising implications for in-country scaling up and capacity building, and broaching conditions under which the approach is most effective.

This monograph is organized into six parts. Part 1 outlines the purpose and the structure of the monograph. Part 2 discusses the positive deviance approach to social change, including the processes and attributes of this strategy. Part 3 describes our methodology and data-collection procedures, including a rationale for employing participatory sketching as a way to give voice to our respondents.

Part 4 describes the Uganda project, including its historic background, the processes involved in implementing the PD approach, and our respondents' perceptions of it expressed in both sketches and narrations. Part 5 describes the Indonesia project, including the pilot study in Village Gadungsari as well as the more recent intervention to use the approach in a larger number of locations to reduce girl trafficking. This part also provides a historic background on both the pilot and the scale-up interventions, including the respective processes involved in implementing the PD approach, and our respondents' perceptions of it expressed in both sketches and narrations. Part 6 distills our conclusions, lessons and recommendations from both sites for using the positive deviance to address child protection issues.

Part 2
The Positive Deviance Approach to Social Change

Can a community solve its problems without requiring a lot of outside resources? Positive deviance is an approach to social change that enables communities to discover the wisdom they already have and then to act on it.[3] The premise is that in every community certain individuals with uncommon practices/behaviors are enabled to find better solutions to problems than their neighbors who have access to the same resources.

The concept of positive deviance gained recognition initially in the work of Tufts University nutrition professor Marian Zeitlin in the 1980s, when she began focusing on why some children in poor communities were better nourished than others.[4] Zeitlin's work privileged an assets-based approach, identifying what was going right in a community in order to amplify it, as opposed to focusing on what was going wrong in a community and fixing it.

Jerry Sternin, a visiting scholar at Tufts University, and his wife, Monique, built on Zeitlin's ideas to organize various PD-centered social change interventions around the world. Some targeted child protection issues, including the two in Uganda and Indonesia that are the focus of this monograph. The Sternins helped institutionalize the PD approach as a social change approach by showing how it could be operationalized as an intervention at the community level.

---

3 Buscell, 8-20; Sternin & Choo, 14-15; Pascale & Sternin, 1-11.
4 Marian Zeitlin, Hossein Ghassemi, And Mohamed Mansour, Positive Deviance in Child Nutrition, (New York: UN University Press, 1990).

To understand the nuances associated with operationalizing PD, a little history is useful. In 1991, the Sternins faced what seemed like an insurmountable challenge in Vietnam. As Director of Save the Children in Vietnam, Jerry was asked by government officials to create an effective, large-scale program to combat child malnutrition and to show results within six months. More than 65 percent of all children living in Vietnamese villages were malnourished at the time. The Vietnamese government realized that the results achieved by traditional supplemental feeding programs were rarely maintained after the programs ended. The Sternins had to come up with an approach that enabled the community to take control of their nutritional status—and quickly.

Jerry Sternin co-pioneer of the Positive Deviance approach in Vietnam

Building on Zeitlin's ideas of PD, the Sternins sought out poor families who had managed to avoid malnutrition without access to any special resources. These families were the positive deviants. They were "positive" because they were doing things right and "deviants" because they engaged in behaviors that most others did not. The Sternins helped the community to discover that mothers in the positive deviant families collected tiny shrimps and crabs from paddy fields and added those with sweet potato greens to their children's meals. These foods were accessible to everyone, but most community members believed they were inappropriate for young children[5]. Also, these PD mothers fed their children three to four times a day, rather than the customary twice a day.

Monique Sternin in Vietnam,
listening as women discussed issues of nutrition

The Sternins created a program through which community members could emulate the positive deviants in their midst. Mothers whose children were malnourished were asked to forage for shrimps, crabs and sweet potato greens and, in the company of other mothers, were taught to cook new recipes that their children ate right there. Within weeks, mothers could see their children becoming healthier. After the pilot project, which lasted two years, malnutrition had decreased by an amazing 85 percent in the communities where the PD approach was implemented. Over the next several years, the PD intervention became a nationwide program in Vietnam, helping over 2.2 million people, including over 500,000

5 Sternin & Choo, 14-15.

18

children, improve their nutritional status.[6]

Social change experts usually make a living discerning the deficits in a community, prioritizing the problems and then trying to implement outside solutions to change them. The positive deviance approach questions the role of outside expertise, believing that the wisdom to solve the problem lies inside. In the approach, the role of experts is to facilitate finding positive deviants, identify the uncommon but effective things that positive deviants do and then make those things visible and actionable.[7] It is led by internal change agents who present the social proof to their peers.[8] Because the PD process amplifies already existing local wisdom, solutions and benefits can be sustained.

The PD approach emphasizes hands-on learning and actionable behaviors.[9] As Jerry Sternin noted, "It is easier to act your way into a new way of thinking than to think your way into a new way of acting".[10] So, the PD approach turns the well-known knowledge, attitude, practice (KAP) framework on its head. As opposed to subscribing to a framework that says increased knowledge changes attitudes, and attitudinal changes change practice, the approach is rooted in changing practice, building on the notion that people change when that change is distilled from

6 Sternin & Choo, 14-15; Monique Sternin, Jerry Sternin, and David Marsh, Scaling up poverty alleviation and nutrition program in Vietnam. T. Machione (ed.), Scaling up, scaling down (Australia: Gordon and Breach Publishers, 1999), 97-117.
7 Richard Pascale, Mark Millemann, and Linda Gioja, Surfing the edge of chaos: The laws of nature and the laws of business (New York: Crown Publishing Groip, 2000).
8 Roger.M. Macklis, "Successful patient safety initiative: Driven from within", Group Practice Journal 50 (2001): 1-5.
9 A positive deviance inquiry focuses on eliminating those client behaviors from the strategy mix that are true but useless (TBU). TBU is a sieve through which a facilitator passes the uncommon qualities of positive deviants to ensure that the identified practices can be practiced by everyone.
10 Dennis Sparks, "From hunger aid to school reform: An interview with Jerry Sternin", Journal for Staff Development (2004): 12-21.

concrete action steps. The box on the following page shows the transcript of part of a launching workshop for the Indonesia project described in this monograph. It illustrates how the PD process is generally facilitated and passed on—staff and *kaders* (village community development workers) own the process and they will share, and eventually cede ownership of the project to their communities.

Evaluations of PD initiatives show that the approach works because the community owns the problem as well as its solutions.[11] The positive deviance approach is now being used to address such diverse issues as reducing childhood anemia, increasing school retention rates, promoting condom use among commercial sex workers and addressing a variety of child protection issues: for instance, reducing female genital cutting in Egypt, curbing the trafficking of girls in Indonesia, and empowering and reintegrating child mothers and vulnerable girl survivors in Northern Uganda.

---

11 See the authors' other writings, particularly, *Positive Deviance Wisdom Series* 1 through 4, published by Boston, Tufts University: Positive Deviance Initiative: #1. Arvind Singhal, Jerry Sternin, & Lucia Dura (2009).   Combating Malnutrition in the Land of a Thousand Rice Fields: Positive Deviance Grows Roots in Vietnam; #2. Lucia Dura and Arvind Singhal (2009). Will Ramon Finish Sixth Grade? Positive Deviance for Student Retention in Rural Argentina; #3. Arvind Singhal, Prucia Buscell, & Keith McCandless (2009). Saving Lives by Changing Relationships: Positive Deviance for MRSA Prevention and Control in a U.S. Hospital; and #4. Arvind Singhal and Lucia Dura (2009). Sunflowers Reaching for the Sun: Positive Deviance for Child Protection in Uganda. www.positivedeviance.org/resources/wisdomseries.html

A Positive Deviance Project Launching Discussion in Gadungsari, West Java

Facilitator (Jerry Sternin): You have highlighted some of the differences and advantages of using the PD approach over your regular approach. Now can you list the most important problems which your village faces?

Various *kaders:* Better life for people in the community...trafficking of girls for the sex trade...poor economy.

Facilitator: Which of these problems do you think is the most serious?

Kaders voting: Trafficking of girls for the sex trade.

Facilitator: Okay. Let's see if we can define the problem very precisely. What is the problem exactly?

Kaders: (after working together for a few minutes in the large group) Many girls from poor families often leave the community and go to work outside and end up in the sex industry.

Facilitator: So, how would we define a PD in the context of this problem?

Kader: A PD would be a poor family who has refused to send their girls out to work in the sex industry.

Kader: A PD would also be a poor family who has made a statement that they absolutely won't send their girls out because they might wind up in the sex industry.

Facilitator: Are there any PDs in this community?

Kader: Yes. Pak Darma is a PD because he has three daughters and is very poor. The youngest daughter recently requested his permission to go to work in Batam (a city near Singapore, well known for being a receiving area for the sex trade). Pak Darma categorically refused her request.

Facilitator: Great example! Are there any other PDs in your village that you know about?

Kader: Yes, there is the case of Pak Samsir. He is very poor but he told me he would never send any of his three daughters out of the village.

Kader: They are not the only ones. I know there are some other poor families who don't or won't send their daughter outside, either. But, we don't know all of them.

Facilitator: Then what do you think we need to do now?

Kader: We should go visit Pak Darma and Pak Samsir.

Facilitator: Why?

Kader: To learn from them.

Facilitator: To learn what?

Kader: To learn their situation.

Facilitator: Oh, you mean what they eat and what are their hobbies?

Kader: No. To learn what enables them to keep their girls at home when other poor families permit their girls to go to far off places to work.

Facilitator: Now, you understand how the positive deviance approach works and how you can use it to help solve the problem of girl trafficking.

Part 3
Methodology and Data-Collection

Our methodology and data-collection procedures to analyze the positive deviance projects on child protection in Uganda and Indonesia, including a distillation of comparative insights and lessons, involved several activities:

1.   We reviewed the existing archival documentation of the positive deviance projects in Uganda and Indonesia, provided to us by Save the Children.

2.   We made field visits to Uganda and Indonesia to gain a contextual understanding of how the positive deviance approach was implemented to address child protection issues in both contexts. In the field, we:

(a) conducted in-depth interviews with key informants—project implementers and managers in Uganda and Indonesia, target beneficiaries, their family members and community leaders and members;

(b) gathered additional secondary data that was available—reports, "change" narratives, photo documentation and the like; and

(c) conducted participatory sketching, our primary data-collection activity, with key informants in both locations.

Participatory Sketching
Participatory visualization techniques have

emerged in recent years as novel, audience-centered and low-cost qualitative methodologies to assess participants' perceptions of, and interpretations about, a social change intervention.[12]

As an example, participatory sketching was employed by one of the authors of this monograph in 2005 to assess the effects of a community-centered intervention in the Peruvian Amazon, spearheaded by Minga Perú, a non-governmental organization that promotes gender equality and reproductive health. One of the questions posed to participants was: "How has my life changed as a consequence of participating in community-based activities of Minga Perú?" Participants were asked to draw two pictures – one to sketch how their life was some five years ago (i.e., *antes*, in the past), and how their life is today (i.e., *ahora*, now).

The *antes* and *ahora* sketches of Emira, a 21-year-old, including her narrative, were highly revealing:

Antes   **Ahora**

Emira noted: "Previously, I was ashamed…sad. Now my personal life has changed. ….I don't feel ashamed any more. [Referring to her breasts….] Now I am proud of my body—my femininity. Before, I didn't

12 Arvind Singhal and Kanta Devi, "Visual Voices in Participatory Communication", Communicator 37, n.2 (2003): 1-15; Arvind Singhal & Elizabeth Rattine-Flaherty, "Pencils and Photos as Tools of Communicative Research and Praxis: Analyzing Minga Perú's Quest for Social Justice in the Amazon", Gazette 68 n.4 (2006): 313-330.

want to cut my hair but now...I cut it. Now I also feel able to wear tight trousers...previously, I wore loose clothes. Also, I wear high heels."

Emira's sketch and its accompanying narrative provided a highly rich, highly poignant and highly textured/nuanced insight on the long-term effects of Minga Perú's interventions in the Peruvian Amazon. Such insights are difficult to gather with the commonly employed personal survey interviews.[13]

Employing participatory sketching activities was especially appropriate in Uganda and Indonesia for a variety of reasons. We were dealing with sensitive, taboo topics (the issue of child mothers and returned abductees in Uganda and girl trafficking in Indonesia) and our respondent populations, who hailed from rural areas, had relatively low levels of literacy (especially in the case of Uganda). Also, participatory sketching allows participants to respond to questions in a non-rushed manner through multiple visual images which, in turn, result in richer and deeper explanations, often wrought with emotion. In comparison, structured interviews are less open-ended and responses to questions are usually less evocative and expressive.

Participatory sketching exercises can help reduce the hierarchical distance between interviewer and interviewee, giving the interviewee more say and control in determining what they believe is salient information. Additionally, the act of narrating one's sketch in front of a group—that is, being on "stage" with a "microphone" and addressing a "captive" audience—is in itself an empowering activity, allowing participants to learn from each others' sketches and narratives.

---

13 Clearly, all methods of data-collection—whether quantitative or qualitative—have their respective strengths and weaknesses.

In Uganda

In Uganda, we worked with seven staff members and associates from the Save the Children's Pader District office to conduct participatory sketching activities with three distinct groups: girls participating in the positive deviance project, their mentors and mothers, and their fathers and local community leaders. The activities took place over two days in two locations: Lukole and Atanga Sub-Counties. Each day, each of the three groups was placed in a separate room of the local schoolhouse for the daylong activities. Over a period of two days, we met with 71 respondents and collected 145 sketches and 145 narrations (Table 1).

Table 1. Breakdown of Data Collection in Uganda

Uganda	Lukole		Atanga		Uganda Totals	
	Respondents	Sketches	Respondents	Sketches	Respondents	Sketches
PD Girls	14	26	12	30	26	56
Menthors/Mothers	16	26	12	18	28	44
Local Leaders/Fathers	10	30	7	15	17	45
Total	**42**	**82**	**31**	**63**	**71**	**145**

The sketching and narrating activities each day, with each set of respondents, lasted between six and seven hours. The following broad questions were posed to the various respondents in Uganda, who were then asked to visualize the responses, sketch them, color them and then narrate them in front of the entire group:

What are various PD practices that the participating girls have learned, adopted and implemented which you believe have made a substantial difference in their life?

How has the life of the young mothers and vulnerable

girls changed as a result of participating in this positive deviance pilot program? What are some visible signs of change in them and in their community?

In Indonesia

In Indonesia, we conducted participatory sketching with 51 respondents and collected 78 sketches and 78 accompanying narrations. Our data-collection activities in Indonesia occurred in two locations: Village Gadungsari, where the positive deviance pilot project to reduce girl trafficking was implemented in 2003, and Village Kedoyo, where the PD project was implemented in 2007 under Save the Children's ENABLE program (explained in greater detail in Part 5 of this monograph).

Table 1. Breakdown of Data Collection in Indonesia

Indonesia	Kedoyo		Gadungsari		Indonesia Totals	
	Respondents	Sketches	Respondents	Sketches	Respondents	Sketches
PD Girls	14	29			14	29
Parents/Kaders	21	22	14	21	35	43
Local Leaders			2	6	2	6
Total	**35**	**51**	**16**	**27**	**51**	**78**

In *Desa* (village) Gadungsari, District Malang, East Java Province of Indonesia, we spent one full working day conducting participatory sketching activities with 16 respondents, of whom 14 were parents of young girls and/or village *kaders*[14] and two were local leaders intimately involved in the implementation or oversight of the PD project on reducing girl trafficking. We hoped to meet with a group of "at-risk-for-trafficking" teenage girls but, as we explain later, they were unable to attend our research sessions due to their scholastic or work

---

14 *Kader* refers to a designated village development workers.

27

commitments—perhaps a sign of the effectiveness of the PD project.

Participatory sketching and narrations with kaders and parents in Gadungsari, East Java, Indonesia

The following broad questions were posed to 16 respondents in Village Gadungsari, who were then asked to visualize the responses, sketch them, color them and then to narrate them in front of the group:

What specific PD practices were identified, adopted and implemented in Gadungsari, that you believe have made a substantial difference in curbing/reducing girl trafficking in your community?

What was Gadungsari like before the PD program was implemented? What is it like today? Describe visible changes by drawing a "Before" and "After" sketch.

We also conducted a three-hour-long interview with Village Secretary Pak Kasmadi, who had guided and championed the PD project since its inception in mid-2003.

In *Desa* (village) Kedoyo, District Tulungagung, East Java Province, we spent one full working day conducting participatory sketching activities with 35 participants divided into two separate groups (each in a different room), including 14 "at-risk-for-trafficking" teenage girls, and 21 parents and/or *kaders* involved in the PD project.

The following broad questions were posed to respondents in Kedoyo:

What specific PD practices were identified, adopted and implemented in Kedoyo that you believe have made a substantial difference in curbing/reducing girl trafficking in your community?

What are some visible changes that you see in Kedoyo since the PD program was implemented?

Sense-Making and Caveats

In overall terms, our data pool from both Uganda and Indonesia comprises 223 sketches and 223 narrations, gathered from 121 respondents.

In both sites, the numbers of sketches and respondents were large enough to allow for a diverse spectrum of responses, as well as provide a rich pool of visual and oral testimonies from which we catalogued and distilled thematic response patterns. This was especially possible because our 121 respondents, comprising target beneficiaries, their parents/family members and community leaders/members, were purposively and carefully selected for their intimate involvement with the PD projects. This purposive selection allowed us to gain rich, process-oriented qualitative insights about how PD behaviors were identified, adopted, and amplified in both research sites.

In Parts 4 and 5 of this monograph, we make sense of the PD projects in Uganda and Indonesia. However, a few caveats are important to voice:

Our exposure to these PD projects is very recent, beginning about mid-July 2008. We spent 17 days in the field from mid-August 2008 to early September 2008: roughly a week on the ground in both Uganda and Indonesia. Prior to our field visits, we spent four to five days reading through the available project documentation and, after the field visits, spent another two weeks or so making sense of our field notes and collected data and writing this monograph. At best, our perspective on these two projects is a view from a galloping Toyota Land Cruiser interspersed with some moments of listening, reflection, and writing.

Our methodology of participatory sketching allows us to convey our perceptions of these projects by presenting and amplifying the rich sketches and insightful narrations of our respondents. Hence, our claims about the PD projects on child protection in Uganda and Indonesia are also necessarily vested in the claims made by our respondents, not amounting to any more, or any less. We have tried to be both rigorous and discerning with our analysis by carefully distilling thematic patterns in our 223 sketches and narrations, while being acutely aware of the boundaries that define and limit our qualitative inquiry.

Although our participatory data-collection activities allow us to provide rich and nuanced descriptive and process-oriented insights (a characteristic of qualitative research), we were not in the realm of posing or testing correlation or causal hypotheses and/or assessing pre-post treatment-control change scores to make (or refute) claims within a certain confidence interval. Qualitative research, even if contextualized with existing archival documentation, can only do so much. It can provide rich insights and answers by especially privileging the "voice" of respondents, the central actors in any social change intervention. So, the sense-making that follows is circumscribed within the qualitative scope of the data gathered and not meant for generalization to other or larger populations groups.

Further, as the case study reports from Uganda and Indonesia in Parts 4 and 5 show, the insights we gained from the participatory sketching exercise were broadly interpreted in conjunction with information gleaned from our in-depth interviews in both locations, as were the archival materials that were made available to us. We especially draw upon the archival materials to describe the two country projects, including the process through which Save the Children implemented them on the ground in cooperation with local partners.

Lastly, where appropriate, Save the Children staff members are identified by their real names. Noted public leaders in our research sites, such as Pak Kasmadi in Gadungsari, Indonesia, are also identified by their real names, but such references are few. None of the other respondents in Uganda or Indonesia is identified by real name to preserve their anonymity. Their names have been changed.

Part 4
Life after the LRA: Piloting Positive Deviance with Child Mothers and Vulnerable Girl Survivors in Northern Uganda

For some 21 years, since 1987, the Lord's Resistance Army (LRA) in Northern Uganda has fought the Ugandan government, uprooted families and homesteads, displaced 2 million people, and killed and maimed tens of thousands of people in a bloody civil conflict. During these years, the LRA abducted an estimated 25,000 to 40,000 children and an equal number of adults.[15] Many of the children abducted by the LRA faced horrors: They were hungry, traumatized, brutalized, raped and held against their will, away from their families and loved ones. Moreover, the LRA forced many of these abducted children—under the barrel of a gun—to kill or maim their family members or neighbors, severing their link with their communities, turning them into outcasts and pariahs.

Since 2006, as the conflict has ebbed,[16] and prospects of peace talks have been broached between the LRA and the Ugandan national government, some thousands of abducted children who survived the LRA passed through government or NGO-run reception centers to be united with their relatives or families living in internally displaced people (IDP) camps. By mid-2008, some 60 percent of those who lived in IDP camps in Northern Uganda had either returned permanently to their original villages or had moved into transitional settlements.[17]

15 Berkeley-Tulane Initiative on Vulnerable Populations. Abducted: The Lord's Resistance Army and forced conscription in northern Uganda. (2007) http://www.reliefweb.int/rw/RWB.NSF/db900SID/EVOD-76JJG5?OpenDocument.
16 The Ugandan army has driven the LRA to retreat to locations in Southern Sudan and North-Eastern fringes of the Democratic Republic of Congo where they are no longer the formidable guerilla force that were in previous years.
17 UNICEF. UNICEF Humanitarian Action update: Uganda, April 25, 2008. http://www.unicef.org/infobycountry/files/Uganda_HAU_Apr08.pdf

In Pader District, inhabited by the Acholi people, the return of internally displaced people to their original homesteads is much slower since the area was most affected by the civil conflict. In Pader District, it was estimated that only 35 percent of the remaining one million IDPs would complete the return to their villages in 2008.[18]

The Positive Deviance Pilot Project

Since March of 2007, Save the Children, with support from the Oak Foundation in Geneva, has implemented a pilot program, *Life after the LRA: Piloting Positive Deviance with the Child Mothers and Vulnerable Girl Survivors in Northern Uganda*, to assist in the empowerment and reintegration process of young mothers and vulnerable girls in Pader District using the positive deviance approach.[19]

The PD project targeted 500 young mothers[20] and vulnerable girl survivors in Pader District as well as 50 adult mentors[21] who provide community-based guidance, monitoring and general psychosocial support. Of the 500 girls, some 40 percent of the girls were identified as formerly abducted child mothers, 50 percent as vulnerable mothers having one or more early pregnancy, and 10 percent as young girls who

18 UNICEF. UNICEF Humanitarian Action update: Uganda, April 25, 2008. http://www.unicef.org/infobycountry/files/Uganda_HAU_Apr08.pdf. For more on the conflict and reintegration in Uganda read: Annan. J, Blattman C., Carlson, K., Mazurana, D. (2008). The state of female youth in Northern Uganda: Findings from the survey of war affected youth (SWAY). The Feinstein International Center. See also
https://wikis.uit.tufts.edu/confluence/display/FIC/The+State+of+Female+Youth+in+Northern+Uganda--Findings+from+the+Survey+of+War+Affected+Youth; Internal Displacement Monitoring Centre (IDMC) (2008). Uganda: Uncertain future for IDPs while peace remains elusive. www.internal-displacement.org; IRIN (2008). Uganda: Optimism prevails despite setback in peace talks. http://www.irinnews.org/report.aspx?ReportId=77823
19 See www.positivedeviance.org.
20 Some 300 young mothers were targeted in 2007 and an additional 200 in 2008.
21 Some 30 mentors in 2007 and 20 mentors in 2008.

served as head of household, responsible for the care of one or more siblings.

The purpose of the pilot project in Northern Uganda was to create an enabling reintegration process for child mothers and vulnerable girl survivors returning from LRA captivity and to reduce their engagement in transactional/commercial sex as a means of survival by strengthening peer support networks, identifying effective and sustainable local solutions for social and economic reintegration, and facilitating access to social services. This was to be accomplished with the aim of:

1.   Identifying livelihood skills support to provide alternative coping mechanisms;

2.   Counseling and mentoring for those who often exhibit extreme antisocial behavior, and who have difficulty reintegrating into their communities;

3.   Developing capacity building strategies in income-generating activities, such as training in basic business skills to meet income needs; and

4.   Creating peer support networks to discuss influential and confidential issues that affect their lives.[22]

Key Project Interventions

Project interventions got underway in March of 2007, beginning with two one-day workshops—one

---

22 Background information provided by Paska Aber, Project Coordinator, Oak
Foundation Project, Save the Children in Uganda.

for district stakeholders and another for sub-county and community stakeholders—and a baseline survey. The survey identified the current living conditions of young mothers and explored their livelihood sources in some detail. At that time, most of the girls engaged in casual labor to survive. This included carrying water to construction sites, selling firewood and collecting grass, as well as the less desirable practice of brewing alcohol. Other girls resorted to transactional sex, *miya wek ami*, for survival.

While agriculture has been the most traditional and stable source of income for the Acholi people, only 20 percent (35 percent of whom were formerly abducted) of the girls who participated in the baseline survey were cultivating agricultural products for their consumption or for sale. This is attributed to the scarcity of land and the cost to buy or rent a plot, about 20,000 shillings (about $12.50, at about 1,600 shillings to the U.S. dollar). This is when earnings per week average roughly 1,000 to 2,000 shillings, and over 80 percent of respondents depend on World Food Program rations for food because the work they do for cash is not dependable.[23]

Community Mapping Activity

With a population of approximately 1,000 "child mothers" and 7,500 vulnerable girls as potential project participants, it was important to identify a manageable target population. Community members did this themselves through the community mapping activities held in five sub-counties over the course of five days in April of 2007.

---

23 Save the Children US. Paska Aber. "Baseline Survey for Save the Children, US on Formerly Abducted Girl Mothers and Other Vulnerable Girls, Pader District, Northern Uganda" (2007).

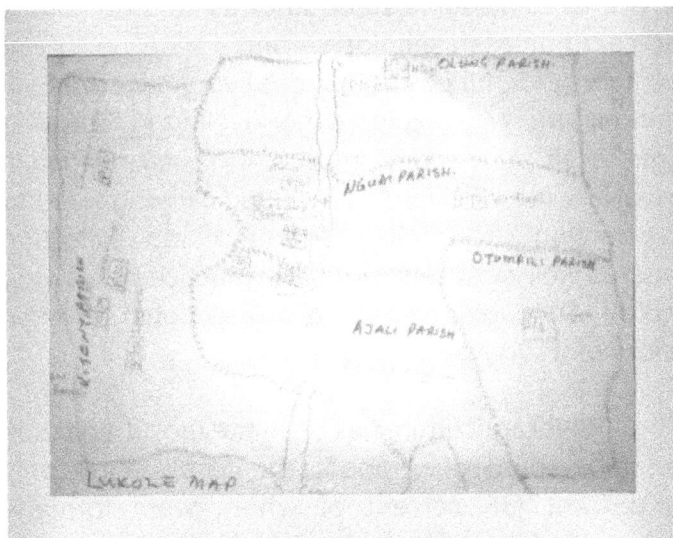

Lukole Sub-County community map
created by the community members

Through mapping activities, 190 potential participants were identified, and physical locations and structures with links to the risk and vulnerability of child mothers and girl survivors were identified and marked on the map itself. This was followed by a discussion of factors leading to young girls' engagement in transactional and commercial sex and possible solutions and alternative coping mechanisms recommended by peers. The map revealed social gathering points, infrastructure, and other relevant information on the girl survivors in the community.[24]

Rapid Assessment—Identification of PD Practices

In the implementation of the PD approach only those behaviors or strategies accessible to all are considered for replication, the rest are deemed "true

---

[24] Save the Children US, Paska Aber, "Report on Community Mapping Exercise" (2007). Also see, Save the Children, Aber, Paska Report on PDI Rapid Assessment (2007).

but useless" and are discarded.[25] A positive deviance inquiry (PDI) team was selected from peer educators, mentors, sub-county representatives and NGO staff members with some PD knowledge undergo a one-day training orientation.

The PD implementation team worked with the community to select the criteria that would be used to identify both PD and non-PD girls. These criteria were based on some unique desirable/undesirable characteristics and practices performed by a few family members and girls in the same social setting within the respective community. Ultimately, in spite of having gone through the hardships of abduction, early pregnancy, being an orphan or being a young head of household, a PD girl would engage in a combination of the following practices:

> working longer and harder than others;
> working collaboratively with others;
> exhibiting self-respect and polite interpersonal behaviors;
> respecting aunts, parents and community elders, and seeking their advice;
> displaying business acumen;
> engaging in crop-growing, selling and other income-generating activities;
> saving money and reinvesting in productive enterprises;
> attending school and performing well.

Once these practices were identified by the community, the girls selected as positive deviants (PD girls) were interviewed in focus groups of two or four in order to arrive at specific coping mechanisms that they believed had worked for them in accomplishing these

25 WebPD Intro. Materials/Bibliography: Presentations (2005) www.positivedeviance.org

practices. For example, in the area of social development, key practices included behavioral changes and healthy relationships. According to PD girls, these were achieved through coping mechanisms like sports, music and exercise. The outcomes then were the behavior adjustments identified in the table below.[26]

Key Practices Related to Social Development	Coping Mechanisms	Outcomes
behavioral changes healthy relationships group work and creativity identification and utilization of alternative coping strategies strong self-resilience psychosocial support self-control and respect marriage	play association with other people sports games music exercise, etc.	awareness of negative behaviors adjusted/reformed behaviors regained self-esteem improved ability to get along with family and community members

After the PD practices were clearly identified, quarterly meetings were held at three different levels: for peer educators, for mentors, and for district officials. Capacity-building trainings were conducted with youth club volunteers (former survivors) and representatives of community-based organizations (CBOs) to enable effective and efficient implementation of project activities.

PD girls discuss issues that affect their lives and possible livelihood activities

---

26 Social development is just one area. More information on socio-economic, education, home and personal hygiene, health practices, and on practices/behaviors identified as non-PD can be found in Paska Aber's Report on PDI Rapid Assessment (2007).

In June 2007, 45 project participants underwent a training session in alternative coping mechanisms in which the main outcome was for them to be able to differentiate the characteristics of positive deviants in the community. By the end of the training, they were able to list and explain the alternative coping mechanism activities that they could replicate and transfer to fellow peers in their community to reduce engagement in transactional sex and address reintegration problems.

In October 2007, 335 participants were divided into two groups for training in basic business and group management. The training equipped them with skills and knowledge to start a business, and engage in income generation activities (IGAs) and self-sustaining initiatives (to initiate, plan, manage, record and evaluate their IGAs and business initiatives and provide customer care). They also learned about ways to manage finances and save some of their income. And, they learned skills that would enable them to develop an interest in and initiate group work to generate income.[27]

Survey Results: One Year Later

I was abducted when I was 9 years old and was attending primary two. I stayed in LRA captivity for 11 years, came back with two children whose father I don't want to talk about because it traumatizes me more. ...I had nasty experiences of bush life; I have big scars of bullet wounds on my legs...but with support from my parents and Save the Children, I have two bags of simsim, two bags of groundnuts, one-and-a-half of sorghum and a cow that has given birth to a

---

27 Save the Children US, Paska Aber, "Piloting the Positive Deviance Approach in Child Protection Intervention", 2007.

calf. These are big achievements in my life. I'm able to buy school uniforms and meet the other needs of my children. I'm committed to hard work and I am rejuvenated.[28]

After the completion of the first year of the PD intervention, Save the Children in Uganda conducted an assessment of the PD pilot project by surveying a representative sample of girl participants.[29] The results of the quantitative survey summarized below showed tremendous progress in terms of understanding, practice and sustainability of identified PD practices and can help us contextualize the results of our participatory assessments.

> **Heightened Awareness**—96.4 percent of project participants said they were aware of the negative effects and consequences of undesirable behaviors such as engagement in transactional sex. Some girls associated their heightened awareness with the replicable PD practices in which they engaged (crop growing, hiring gardens, savings from "cash for work" communal work, IGAs, selling in the markets, small shops, etc.) despite the social, physical, psychological and sociocultural difficulties they faced. Some PD girls believed going back to school helped their social development and resilience. Others believed psychosocial support, in the form of counseling and cognitive therapy, was key to their awareness.
>
> **Enhanced Self-Concept**—96.4 percent of girls said they regained self-respect and self-esteem

---

28 Pilot project participant quoted in Save the Children in Uganda First Year Assessment Report under "Case Studies."
29 Save the Children in Uganda, Luc Vanhoorickx, Paska Aber, S.L. Odong. Positive deviance with vulnerable girls—first year assessment report, (2008).

from relationships with mentors and their participation in recreational activities such as games, dance and drama.

Improved Hygiene—98.2 percent of girls appeared clean, as did their environment. The walls and floors of their homes were smeared regularly—a task they used to leave to their mothers because "we thought it was dirty smearing the house every time and looking for cow dung...."[30] They said regular washing of clothes and bedding was important, especially when one had a baby, and bathing two or three times a day, especially after a heavy workload, was essential.

Lanyut Maber— Aspirations for being a Role Model—92.7 percent said they had been identified as "role models" by their community members, mentors and peers. One of the participants said, *"ber kit loyo lonyo"*—being well-behaved is better than wealth. She added that being a role model was sometimes underrated or taken for granted, but should be valued as a special trait that helps with rehabilitation and reintegration.

Enhanced Social Engagement —92.7 percent of participants said they had been involved in the design and facilitation of discussions, debates, sharing, and storytelling about sensitive subjects. 94.5 percent said they were actively involved in all activities relevant to the project.

---

30 Pilot project participant quoted in Save the Children in Uganda First Year Assessment Report under "Results."

Participants leading the design and implementation of PD project activities

Return to Education—Only 7.3 percent of girls who participated in the project in 2007 decided to practice the PD behavior of going back to school as a way of improving their reintegration and reducing their engagement in transactional sex as a means of survival.

Adoption of Crop Growing and Animal Rearing—92.7 percent of participants engaged in crop growing and 47.3 percent had bought domestic animals such as pigs, goats, and even cows.

Pursuing Small Business Opportunities —36.4 percent of girls chose *awaro*, or market vending, as their primary business. 10.9 percent of girls engaged in mobile produce sale such as operating a small business store. 5.5 percent of girls chose to capitalize on the accessibility of roads next to the IDP camps to set up food joints.

Saving Practices—53.8 percent of girls reported savings of above 50,000 shillings (about $31.25) after the first year. This number is significant, especially when considering that the inputs for this project ranged from 60,000 to 70,000 shillings (about $37.5 to $43.75) per person.

The survey results, consistently positive, strongly reinforce the patterns that merged in the participatory sketching activity, providing contextual validation to the outcomes described in the next section.

Results of Participatory Sketching

As noted previously, our participatory sketching activities in Uganda were carried out with three groups of respondents—PD girls, mentors and mothers, and local community leaders and fathers—in Lukole and Atanga Sub-Counties. Its purpose was to gain a richer understanding of *the process* through which PD practices were identified, adopted, and implemented by the target beneficiaries (the young mothers and vulnerable girl survivors), and the resulting changes in their lives.

PD Practices Adopted by Young Mothers in Northern Uganda

The young mothers and vulnerable girls participating in the project in Northern Uganda and their mentors, parents, and community members identified several PD practices that they believed had made a big difference in socioeconomically empowering the girls. By itself, adoption of any one PD practice might not have amounted to much, but taken together, they had significantly improved the quality of life of these girls, earning them respect within their larger community and, in some instances, even envy.

One of the project mentors in Atanga Sub-County, Grace, who worked closely with 12 young girls and was affectionately referred to as the "mother of the camp," drew a simple seven-point sketch to talk about the various PD practices that were making a substantial difference in the lives of these girls.

Grace's seven-point sketch outlining specific PD practices that had empowered vulnerable girls

She noted:

In this sketch, first you can see that the vulnerable girls are now getting together to talk. They hold regular meetings among themselves, with me, and with Paska and Simon [members of the Save the Chidren PD implementing team in Pader District]. In these meetings, they learn new things and find strength in each other's company. Second, almost all the girls who work with me have built their own house to sleep in. They find dignity and self-respect in having their own place. Third, these girls have many productive income-generating activities. For instance, they raise chickens and have gardens in which they grow different types of crops. Some of what they grow, they consume. The rest they sell to earn money. This money is then invested in other business enterprises and also put in a savings bank where it earns interest. Fourth, some girls [3 out of 12] have bought their own bicycles that they ride to schools, to markets and to attend meetings. Fifth, these girls have good social habits. [Pointing to her sketch….] They greet people respectfully. They wear clean clothes. They take care of their hygiene and their babies. Sixth, all girls have water pots in which they store drinking water. They cover it to keep away dust, flies and insects. Seventh, these girls have now begun to plant quick-growing vegetables like onions, tomatoes, beans and cucumbers. Unlike millet, simsim and groundnut, these plants grow fast. They consume some of these vegetables and sell the rest in their neighborhood or in the market." Grace beamed with pride as she wrapped up her narration, and said, "I can go on and on. But I must stop!"

Abby, the mother of one of the young mothers in Lukole Sub-County, elaborated on certain PD practices that her daughter had adopted. Pointing to her sketch, with tears swelling in her eyes, Abby recalled that her daughter had become pregnant when she was 13, bringing shame to the family and dropping out of school.

Abby's sketch emphasizing how her daughter works hard and manages her time between school, business and child care

Pointing to her sketch, Abby continued:

After participating in Save the Children's PD project, my daughter is now back in school. She works very hard and her teachers praise her. On school days, she returns home during the morning break to breastfeed her child, who is under my care. During the lunch break, she rides her newly acquired bicycle to the market to see if there is any produce she can buy cheaply to sell at a profit. On the non-school days, she attends to her garden. She uses her time well. She realizes 'time is money'. She plans her daily life, focusing on what needs to be done at that moment. She is not lazy. I am proud of the way she takes care of her baby. She is by far a better mother than I was.

Grace and Abby's list of PD practices are, not surprisingly, consistent with the list of PD behaviors identified during the community-led PD inquiry, some 15 months previously. That is, a PD girl:

works longer and harder than others,

works collaboratively with others,

- exhibits self-respect and polite interpersonal behaviors,

respects aunts, parents and community elders, and seeks their advice,

displays business acumen,

engages in crop-growing, selling and other income-generating activities,

saves money and reinvests in productive enterprises,

attends school and performs well.

The one point of departure between the survey data and the qualitative findings lies in the number of girls who had returned to school. The February–March 2008 survey data showed that only 7.3 percent of the PD girls were attending school, where as our qualitative research seemed to suggest that perhaps school attendance was more widespread (based on the patterns observed in the sketches and narrations). Some possible explanations for this may be that in the five–six months between the survey and this qualitative research, the number of girls returning to school may have increased in some locations. It could be that the 7.3 percent figure in the survey could have been disproportionately contributed by the PD girls in Lukole and Atanga Sub-Counties. Or perhaps there were other contributory factors.

The qualitative research, nevertheless, validated that the PD behaviors that were purposely amplified by the project repeated themselves with regularity in our respondents' sketches and narrations. In so doing, they provided an even more nuanced understanding of how they were put into practice.

Works Harder, Smarter and Together

Edmond, father of one of the PD girls in the Lukole sub-county, emphasized, "The PD girls work in their gardens whenever they can find time. When not in school, they work all through the morning. And while most other women return home for other domestic chores or rest, many PD girls return back to their gardens in the afternoon or evening."

PD girls working collaboratively in their gardens

PD girls work harder and smarter by practicing a variety of behaviors. Jane, one of the PD girls, added, "After finishing work in my garden, I work in other community members' fields to earn extra money." Marie, another PD girl said, "If I dig in a mango garden, I bring back some mangoes to eat or sell." Grace, a mentor, noted, "When they go to fetch firewood some girls bring back an extra load. One they use for cooking, the other they sell or use the next day. One girl makes extra money by filling up an additional jerry-can of water at the hand pump, strapping it behind her bicycle and delivering it to a construction site."

Anna, a project mentor in Atanga Sub-County, emphasized the importance of the support that the girls provide to each other, "The girls are unified. They

trust each other. They work hard. They play hard."
Madeline, a mother of one of the PD girls, agreed. "I see
many of these girls work together. If one has a big field,
it can be boring to work alone. The job looks very big.
But when you are together, you have a good time, and
the work finishes quickly. When girls are planting or
tilling, they often do it by working in rows [pointing to
her sketch]. No one wants to be out of step—or left
behind."

Several sketches and narrations emphasized the
group-based PD practices of PD girls. Anna, Kit and
Anna, collectively drew the sketch below and provided
the following narration:

A collective sketch about group practices

"After our capacity-building training with Save
the Children, we began sharing information about what
crops to grow. We worked in the field together and
gathered our produce and together sold it in the
market. Now we have bought goats together and, if
they reproduce in good number, we will divide the
earnings among ourselves."

Gladys pointed to another PD group practice: "We send somebody to sell one week and another person the next week — we take turns. This way we can avoid duplication of effort and use our time productively."

Ebony, another mentor, emphasized how this group identity builds norms of reciprocity and social cohesion: "The girls visit each other. They socialize. They believe they share a common bond and are part of something bigger than themselves."

Adela, a mentor in Lukole, emphasized the importance of group singing and dancing in building a sense of unity among the girls. Pointing to her sketch, she noted:

> These girls love to perform the *larakaraka*, the vigorous and sensuous Acholi courtship dance. They dance it wearing their colorful *kikoyi* skirts and Save the Children T-shirts. And, you can see there is a 'commander' in front guiding the girls, blowing a whistle and another girl playing the drums. Beating the drums and the kalabash are typically roles ascribed to men in the Acholi culture. But these girls now hold their head high in the community and can do anything. Yes, anything.

Adela's sketch of PD girls dancing the *larakaraka*

Nancy's sketch showing a game of netball
with her peers as psychosocial therapy

The PD girls also repeatedly emphasized the therapeutic value of engaging in peer-centered group activities. For example, playing netball on a regular basis was identified by many girls in Atanga sub-county as a PD group practice. When asked why that was the case, Nancy, a young former abductee and mother, responded, "When we are feeling sad or depressed instead of sulking alone we look for peers, and often this takes the form of joining a game of netball."

Respects Oneself and Others; Seeks Advice

Mentors and parents of girls participating in the PD project emphasized the girls' improved self-concept, interactional behavior, and social skills. As Robina, mother of a young mother, noted:

Initially, my girl was a problem child. After participating in the program, she has learned good behaviors and manners. She is now respectful to me and polite to others. She is confident and self-assured but yet asks for my advice about what to plant or sell. Every evening she comes back home directly from the market with money in her hand. She does not stop in a disco or in a bar. And, she always brings me a soda.

Rachel, another mother whose daughter is a participant in the PD project, noted, "Now my daughter kneels down when she talks to me. Previously, I had a 'monster' in my house. Now I have a human being."

Rachel's sketch depicting her daughter's respectful behavior

Several mentors and mothers in both Lukole and Atanga sub-counties talked about the important role of faith and church-going in "calming the minds" of these young mothers—many of whom had returned from captivity and faced stigma and discrimination from community members. Grace, a mentor and herself a devout Christian, noted, "Many of these girls now go to church. This renews their faith in the almighty, even if they faced cruelty, abuse and trauma in captivity. Their faith gives them hope and courage. It gives them ground to stand on. They learn that by hard work, forgiveness and love, they can attain salvation."

Rachel, another mentor, noted, "The girls dress well when they go to church." Pointing at her sketch, she continued:

Rachel's sketch emphasizing the important role
of the church in the lives of girls

In our church, the preacher advises these girls not to become pregnant early and to focus on their studies. He also cautions young boys to study hard and behave well. This way all in the community would be healthy and lead a fulfilling life. Many of these girls now sing in church choir. Also, in church the girls and boys have conferences under the guidance of elders so they can remain strong and out of trouble. It is here that they learn about the importance of self-respect and respect for others.

Several mentors talked about the respect that the PD girls bestow on them in various ways. Abby noted, "Girls come to me for all kinds of advice, and especially about what to do with the money they have earned. I give them advice about buying and selling, and also tell them about the importance of saving money in the bank so it could earn interest. They listen to me. They look upon me as a 'mother,' and follow my advice carefully."

Abby's sketch showing how PD girls
follow her advice

Anna, another mentor, agreed: "The girls are very respectful. I see my mentor role as being one of a chameleon. I am aware of what they are doing. But I do not interfere. I keep a close watch from the sideline." The girls in Anna's care characterized their mentor's style as one who "Talks less and does more. And, one who leads by example."

Displays Business Acumen, Saves, Invests, and Learns

Our respondents' sketches and narrations provided rich insights about the business skills acquired and practiced by the PD girls with respect to planning, budgeting, prioritizing, saving and investing. Girls also value being in school and continued learning. Angela, a PD girl wearing smart boots and standing by her newly purchased bicycle, shared her business wisdom: "When I go to the market I am not only selling.... With the profits from my business I am also buying. When other girls come to ask me for advice, I tell them to take every bit of money they have and invest it diversifying their range of income-generating activity." Further, Angela told us that she has saved more than 200,000 shillings ($125), a big sum of money in rural Uganda. Her short-term plan is to buy a plot of land and construct a decent hut.

Sixteen-year-old Aber's multiprong entrepreneurship practices in Lukole sub-county are also noteworthy:

With the small money I received, I hired a sewing machine. Now I'm repairing and selling secondhand clothes. I have made some sales and I have the money in my pocket. I have three sacks of maize saved from my garden, and I also have another garden in which I grow eggplant and other vegetables. I have hired a boy who helps sells in the market. My business is going well. Here I am sitting with my child at home relaxing. Now I can take tea (pointing to the big cup). I have enough money to buy sugar.

Aber with her child enjoying a cup of tea

Other girls in Pader District have adopted several seemingly small but critical buying and selling PD behaviors. For instance, Rachel noted that she learned "…the importance of spreading the produce on a raised platform instead of on the ground; and to arrange products in piles and/or bunches." Also, pointing to her sketch, Rachel emphasized, "By putting price tags on my products, I avoid haggling and sell the produce for a fair price."

PD girl selling produce on a platform in
neat piles with price tags

Angela added, "First these girls just sold fresh produce. Now they add value to it and make a higher profit. For instance, here is a girl who roasts bananas, corn and groundnuts. She can then sell these products at three times the price. Also, many girls have begun to make and sell lagalagala, small baked breads made out of mashed cassava, banana and sugar."

Roasting bananas, corn, and groundnuts
to add value to a product

Some PD girls, either on their own or collaboratively with their peers, hire a neighbor to serve as babysitter for their children when they work in the gardens or when they go to the market for selling.

Jowi noted, "By babysitting, my neighbor earns some money, and also it allows us to work longer in our gardens or to sell until later in the market. This way we can increase our profits. Also, we have noticed that this increases the bond between me and my daughter. I am less irritated at her. She is also happy to see me after a long day."

Many PD girls now are planning for their future and of their children. They are also prioritizing, budgeting, saving and investing as per a plan. As Angela noted:

With my savings, I will buy a bull. Then I can rent an ox plow and till and plant a bigger piece of land. I can also invest some money to hire labor for digging and weeding, and plant groundnuts, simsim and sunflower—crops that give higher profits. Perhaps in a few years, I will be able to buy the ox plow and would not need to rent it. Then I can use it in my fields and also rent to others, recovering my investment and making more money.

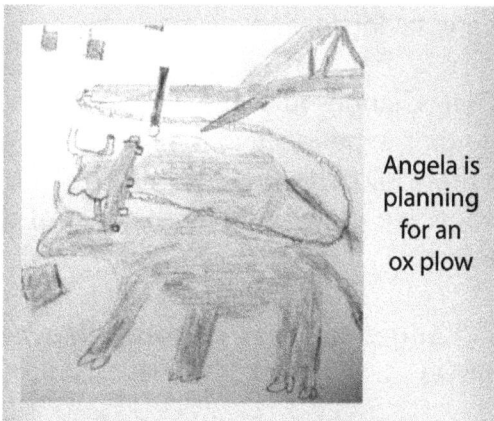

Angela is planning for an ox plow

For many of the PD girls in Pader District of Northern Uganda, an important part of planning for the future involves an investment in their own learning. This means many have either returned to school or are planning to do so. The simple act of returning to school brings into sharp focus the self-reinforcing, virtuous interconnections between a wide variety of PD practices that the young mothers and vulnerable girls have acquired and adopted.

So, in conclusion, what are the various PD practices that the participating girls have learned, adopted and implemented which have made a substantial difference in their life?

Abby's sketch, early on in this section, about her daughter's balancing of school, work and child care aptly summarizes the various PD behaviors that were adopted by the PD girls. As Abby emphasized, returning to school requires saving money, managing one's time judiciously, working hard and collaboratively, having harmonious relations with mentors, parents and other community members, going to church, taking care of one's child, working in the garden, selling in the market, investing the proceeds and saving for a better tomorrow.

What changes did the young mothers and vulnerable girls experience in their lives as a result of adopting these PD behaviors and practices? To answer this question, we draw upon another set of sketches and narrations.

Positive Changes in Lives of Young Mothers and Communities

The young mothers and vulnerable girls participating in the PD program in Northern Uganda and their mentors, parents and community members reflected on how involvement in the PD program had helped in bringing positive changes in the life of the girls and the community. While substantial progress had been made in socioeconomically empowering the young and vulnerable mothers as well as the returned abductees, certain challenges remained to be resolved and deserved ongoing intervention and attention.

One of the PD mothers in Atanga Sub-County, Alice, drew the following sketch to graphically summarize the changes experienced by her daughter after participating in the PD program, saying, "For the first early years of her life, my daughter was a good person. I have drawn her on the left in green color as that depicts a person who is leading a natural, organic, earthy and healthy life."

Alice's daughter: From "monster" to "divine"

Alice continued:

Then during the conflict my daughter was abducted. It was a very painful moment for the family. She stayed in the bush for four years, and we had no idea whether she survived or not. It was no fault of hers but when she came back from captivity, her behavior was appalling. She was like a monster. [Pointing to the red area in her chest and in her head depicting "evil"]…she came back with a distrustful heart and mind. She was disrespectful and aloof and lazy. She did not want to work in the field or return to school. She went to discos. To survive, she engaged in *miya wek ami* "give and take," referring to transactional sex. But after involvement in the program she has gone over time from being a "monster" to being "divine" (back to green color). She works hard, is polite, is making money the right way. She is also saving and investing, and back in school. She also works very well with other girls.

Physical, Material and Psychological Well-Being

Without exception, the sketches and narrations of the participating PD girls emphasized the radical improvement that had occurred in their quality of life. Although Acholi culture professes modesty and humility, the girls are proud of their accomplishments under difficult and trying circumstances. Their narratives and sketches reflect their present empowered state of physical, material and psychological well-being.

Sylvia drew the following sketch and proudly narrated, "I now have a big house. It is well-furnished with plastic chairs, and the table has a table linen. I have bathing soap, toothbrush, toothpaste and oil for smearing. I have a bag with money inside. I am wearing shoes and nice clothes. I also have chickens."

Sylvia's sketch depicting her altered life

Pointing to the broom in her hand, Sylvia continued, "I now sweep the compound twice daily. My community has a bath shelter, a latrine and a washing basin, which we use after using the toilet. We have a tree outside my home and when my friends come to visit we sit under the shade on the mat. We talk and rest."

Sylvia's narration deserves elaboration. Having a table means that she does not have to eat off of the floor, much less serve visitors on the floor. The reference to wearing a dress, carrying a handbag with money inside, and shoes with socks are signs of personal success and a sense of self-worth. The mention of a toilet, a latrine, a washing basin indicates changes in health, hygiene and sanitation norms within the community. These changes are amplified by her personal reference to sweeping the compound, and using bathing soap and a toothbrush.

Further, Sylvia's reference to sitting under the tree on a mat has tremendous symbolic meaning in Acholi culture. Among the Acholi of Northern Uganda, having a tree next to one's homestead is significant at various levels. It is a place where elders sit with authority, a sense of well-being and composure to tell stories. A mat signifies a place of rest, a place of greeting, a sign of welcome. The tree and the mat were ubiquitous in the PD girls' change-narratives as evidenced by their portrayal in other sketches.

The ubiquitous tree and the mat in several sketches

Below, in Betty's sketch, we also see a sense of physical, material and psychological well-being. Betty's narration allows us to understand how she views her personal transformation.

Betty's many possessions, including
the clothesline to hang clothes

Betty noted:

Before I joined I was a very tiny girl—now I've even put on weight. I was sleeping in a very tiny house and cooking in that tiny house. Later I felt I had the strength to build a bigger house. In my big house, I have a bed and a curtain. I am eating; you can see my food. I can even sit on my mat under the shade. I have a tray to wash and dry my utensils. I have an *agulu* (water pot) to store and cool water and a wire to hang clothing; I even have a jerry-can. I do work for cash—here you can see money (she traced two gold-colored coins next to her head). I now budget and plan.

Betty's sketch and narration also deserve elaboration. Betty draws herself on the right as a very tiny girl, and in the center of the sketch she shows us her robust growth and the strength she gained to build a bigger house. Her social growth is evidenced by her

63

explicit mention of being able to sit on her mat under the shade of the tree. For Betty, physical and material well-being and hygiene is symbolized in the tray where she washes and dries her utensils as well as in the wire where she can hang her clean clothes to dry. Akin to the ubiquitous mat under the tree, many girls drew and talked about the wire to hang clothing. They were quick to point out that a wire symbolizes several pairs of clothes for them and their child, material well-being, social status, personal hygiene, grooming, and self-respect.

Roseline's sketch and narrative also depict the physical, material and psychological changes in her life, and includes a reference to the clothesline. "When I gave birth, I didn't have any clothing for my child. I tore my skirt in half to put the baby on my back. After Save the Children came to my community, I used the money well, worked hard and was able to buy clothes for my baby. Here you see them drying on the clothesline."

Roseline's sketch depicts a transformation from a focus on survival and basic needs to an appreciation for aesthetics

"Before participating in this program, I used to bathe my child in a calabash. Now I use a plastic basin. Earlier, I used to be a very notorious girl. Now I am well-plaited and groomed. I have a garden and flowers in front of my house."

Roseline's transformation is illustrated by owning one set of clothes—those she was wearing—to several pairs that she now washes and hangs. Roseline's sketch focused on a few material objects that make a big difference in her daily life, and she drew them large, with bold lines and strong colors. Her narration shows the move from a focus on basic needs to an appreciation for aesthetics. Her eyes sparkled when she talked about "how nice it is to be surrounded by beautiful, colorful flowers."

In Peggy's sketch, we again see the clothesline, the tree, her nice dress and shoes, a table and chair, and some other material objects that signify her sense of well-being.

Peggy's sketch depicting her well being

She further elaborated, "I bought a radio to give me information from the outside world. For my child, I bought a cap and a shirt so that he looks smart in the community.

Peggy is not alone in wanting to have material possessions, such as a radio, that may seem luxurious in her surroundings. But their significance goes beyond the lure of material goods to a deep personal sense of dignity and self-worth that keeps girls like Peggy from engaging in miya wek ami or commercial sex.

Gladys concurred: "I used to visit disco bars to see if I could get money from men. I did not want to be seen or identified with my child because it would spoil my social evenings. But Save the Children's program gave me strength and support and I started working on my own. I used to steal from people's gardens but now I have my own things. I used to fight so much but now I am a law-abiding person."

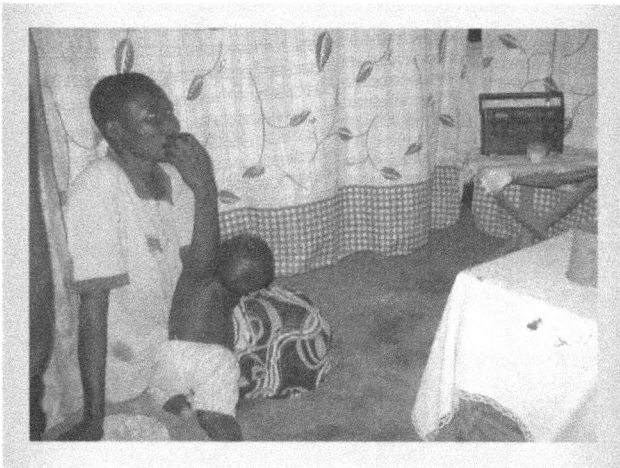

Abby in her home, proudly displaying a curtain dividing the sleeping area, a table with a table cloth, a cup, smearing oil, and a radio

Several PD girls in their sketches emphasized

that their return to school and their attendance in the local church has helped "calm their minds." Several mothers and mentors also strongly reinforced the role that the girls' Christian faith has played in their attempts to lead a virtuous life, including love for neighbors, forgiveness, dignity, and hard work.

Business Success, Role Modeling and Social Integration

The sketches and narrations of the participating PD girls, their mentors, and parents highlighted how entrepreneurship and business skills, coupled with time and money management, have raised their social standing in the community. Many are hailed as role models.

Janice, for instance, not only achieved business success through her hard work and initiative, but generously provides financial advice to other members of the community. Through the following sketch and narration Janice elaborated on her business practices and how that has raised her social standing among her peers and in community circles.

Janice's business and social success as depicted in her sketch

Janice noted:

The amount of cash that I got from Save the Children was small. After receiving the money, I sat down and drew a budget. I took part of the money and used it for growing crops, and with what I was able to produce and sell, I bought some land. But I then was short of cash, so I had to adjust my plans. But I worked hard and had 12 extra sacks of groundnuts the next year. When I sold it, I received a lot of money and bought a cow—you can see it in the picture. Next year I will buy a bull so I can use a ox-plow and plant a bigger garden. You can see in the drawing I have good clothing. Before [pointing to the top left], I was a very bad girl [in red color]; now I am a role model [in the center in green color]. …Now I am respected in the village. I meet doctors who bring medicine to children—I serve as a resource person for health in the community. I like being with my peers. Before we used to only think about transactional sex for that was the only way to survive, and now I don't even dream of it.

For Janice to be able to buy a plot of land and a cow in 15 months shows her extraordinary grit, hard work and business acumen. The cow alone cost her about $200, nearly five times the amount of seed money she was provided by Save the Children.

Ellen's narration and sketch echoed Janice's sentiments about feeling valued in the community for her business and creative acumen and how with the new bicycle and increased visibility and mobility, her social standing has gone up even further.

Ellen's business skills, bicycle and vented
toilet are highly visible in her community

Ellen explained:

I have simsim and maize in my garden. I have a
bicycle for myself that I can ride far to buy and sell
products. I now have a toilet...it is not smelly
because I've put an external pipe on it. I am not
embarrassed to bring my friends home now.
[Brimming with a mix of modesty and pride, she
noted in a low voice] ....I am considered a model—a
PD girl whose behavioral practices one can learn
from. Mothers of my friends and community
members point to me saying, "Be like her." Also, I do
not have a second child, while most of my peers do.
People now say, "Eh, Save the Children has done
well for this girl."

What is remarkable about Ellen's narration is the
motivation she brings to go beyond the minimum
expectations for survival and reintegration. She is not
aiming to be simply accepted, and she is already in a
place where she is worthy of emulation.

Sylvia's sketch and narration amplifies her accomplishments as well as those of other PD girls in northern Uganda. In her sketch (below), we notice that her circular house is clearly compartmentalized with curtains into different areas for living, storing, entertaining and sleeping.

Sylvia's commentary on reintegration: from "me to we"

Sylvia said:

When I joined the PD program, I used the money for buying and selling fruits. Here I have drawn myself coming from the market. In my house I have everything. I have tomatoes, silverfish even cups. In that house I also store food—I have three sacks of groundnuts. I have my bedding and a mat. I have even designed and decorated the house. I have curtains and a tablecloth—the house is beautiful. I have a long elevated stool that I use in the market to put products on. I also have one chicken with six chicks and a goat. In my garden, the millet crops are yielding very well. Before I joined the program, I was isolated in the community. Not too many people talked to me. Now I stay with my peers, fellow girls, and my community. We share ideas and experiences. We do community work together.

Most striking in Sylvia's narration is the last part in which she transitions from talking about her as "me" to talking about "we" signifying a sense of social well-being. She expresses her joy in no longer being isolated, making explicit reference to being integrated with her peers and community.

Cumulatively, our respondents' sketches and narrations suggest that great strides have been made in the reintegration of former abductees, child mothers and vulnerable girls into mainstream Acholi society, which in itself is inching toward a semblance of stability and rebuilding after a violent civil conflict. In such a societal context, the lives of these child mothers and vulnerable girls have been markedly "jump started" by Save the Children's PD program, leading to an interesting dialectic of both adulation and envy for the participating girls. On one hand, community members admire the empowered girls, and on the other, there is jealousy.

As Joyce, one of the mothers of a PD girl, emphasized, "The PD girls are role models. They are respectful and resourceful. They wear clean clothes and have food on the table. They work hard and have taken control of their lives. So, here we can see a community member welcoming the PD girls back to the community, asking them about their meeting and shaking their hands." Thus, the pendulum of integration, as per Joyce, if anything, had swung back to normalcy, if not tipped over.

Joyce continued, "Other parents in the community and other girls who have not participated in this program are jealous of these girls [pointing to their red-colored hearts]. They feel that these girls were singled out by Save the Children for support. 'What about other children in the community?' they ask."

Jealousy for PD girls among community members

Many other parents and mentors concurred with Joyce's concern. A community elder in Lukole asked, "What about boys who have returned from captivity? Why is Save the Children not helping them?" One mentor said, "What about other girls who are not pregnant who are struggling in school or falling into bad company? Why not programs for them?"

When we asked how this jealousy could be addressed constructively, several community members provided suggestions. One mother said, "Each girl who is participating in the PD program should be partnered with another girl in the community, so she could also be part of the support network and learn business and other social skills from a peer model." Another community elder suggested, "What is taught to the mentors by Save the Children should also be taught to other mothers in the community. Alternatively, each mentor should mentor four or five mothers to become mentors to their daughters, nieces and other community children." In essence, the operative suggestion was "joint ventures" between the PD girls, mentors and mothers and their respective counterparts in the community.

Conclusion

How did the life of the young mothers and vulnerable girls change as a result of participating in this positive deviance pilot program? And what are some visible signs of change in their communities?

The sketches and narrations show that the participating PD girls experienced a marked improvement in their quality-of-life. Those who participated in the pilot PD project, in general, exuded an empowered state of physical, material and psychological well-being. The sketches and narrations also suggest that the entrepreneurship and business skills that the girls gained as a result of participating in the program, coupled with time and money management skills they acquired over time, helped elevate their social standing in the community.

However, the adulation for the PD girls is also not without envy. Community members admire the empowered PD girls but are also jealous as they believe that other boys and girls in the community, who also are highly vulnerable, will either be left behind or fall through the societal safety nets.

Part 5
Positive Deviance to Reduce Trafficking of Young Girls in East Java, Indonesia

With the prospects of earning an average income of less than Rp. 5,000 (about 75 cents) per day in some rural areas, and with the tacit acceptance of sex work as a viable form of employment, many girls and women from East Java, Indonesia, leave their villages and often seek employment in the sex or entertainment industry.[31]

In 2000, an estimated 30 to 40 percent of all commercial sex workers in Indonesia were under 18 years of age, suggesting a high incidence of girl trafficking. To address this problem, Save the Children, with support from the Oak Foundation, piloted an anti-trafficking program in partnership with the East Java Institution for Community Research and Development (*Lembaga Pelesenan Kenderaan Perdagangan*, abbreviated as LPKP). The program, which ran from December 2002 to February 2005, aimed "to reduce the number of girls trafficked into the sex industry through appropriate and sustainable grassroots anti-trafficking initiatives."[32] While the program was piloted in three villages of East Java, its success is especially well documented in Village Gadungsari.

Here we provide a background on the positive deviance project to reduce girl trafficking in Indonesia by discussing the Save the Children's pilot experience and its expansion and scale-up to another 100

---

31 The figure cited is from Titing Martini, "PD for girl trafficking prevention: Experience from south Malang." PD Bulletin 1 no. 4 (2005). http://www.positivedeviance.org/materials/publications.html. See also Save the Children—IFO (2005). Brief information on Save the Children-IFO trafficking prevention program. Provided by SC as background information.

32 Save the Children—IFO. Brief information on Save the Children-IFO trafficking prevention program (2005). Provided by SC as background information.

communities in East Java. Our primary data-collection activities in Indonesia were based in two sites: Village Gadungsari in District Malang, where the PD project was piloted in 2003, and Village Kedoyo in District Tulungagung, where Save the Children began to use the positive deviance approach in April 2007 as part of the ENABLE (Enabling Communities to Combat Child Trafficking through Education) project, which we describe later.

The PD Project Gets Under Way in Gadungsari

In May of 2003, positive deviance expert/consultant Jerry Sternin facilitated a workshop in Village Gadungsari, District Malang, East Java Province, to provide *kaders* (or designated village-level development workers) and LPKP staff a deeper understanding of the positive deviance approach. While the issue of girl trafficking had been identified as a problem facing Gadungsari, given the taboo nature of the topic, the PD session was framed as a forum to address community problems in general.[33] The workshop, as described in the box in Part 2 of this monograph, identified girl trafficking as a major issue.

Community Mapping

Working closely with Pak Kasmadi, the Village Secretary of Gadungsari, and representatives of LPKP, the local partner NGO, the kaders developed a strategy of consolidating community support slowly and carefully. They decided that the traditional PD kick-off meeting, where community members come together

---

[33] This information and the text that follows were taken and summarized or excerpted from: Jerry Sternin (2003). Transcription of workshop/meeting with LPKP staff and village kaders. The full transcription of the 3 hour and 45 minute session is available on the Positive Deviance webpage:
http://www.positivedeviance.org/projects/indgirltraffick/kaders_workshop.pdf

to define the problem and commit to addressing it, was far too risky for the trafficking issue. The meeting would have to wait until the team had laid the groundwork by gathering first with individual families to discuss the gravity of the situation in the village. Only when they were assured of sufficient support and had forged strong enough interpersonal and group alliances, could they go public with the campaign to curb trafficking.

Kaders in Indonesia at a PD training[34]

In the weeks after the PD workshop, the kaders made a simple map of the entire village, circling the homes of those girls that were missing from the village and those most at risk for trafficking. The mapping exercise opened their eyes about the extent of girl trafficking occurring in Gadungsari.

Some 50 people in Gadungsari participated in the community mapping activity, and its results were startling. The mapping exercise revealed that roughly 140 people were missing from the village, 90 percent of

34 Photograph from Positive Deviance Initiative webpage: http://www.positivedeviance.org/projects/indgirltraffick/

whom were young girls 14 to 17 years old.[35] Mapping was also used to visually depict how power was distributed through the twelve hamlets in Gadungsari, what level of influence was wielded by which trafficker on what residents and why, and so on.

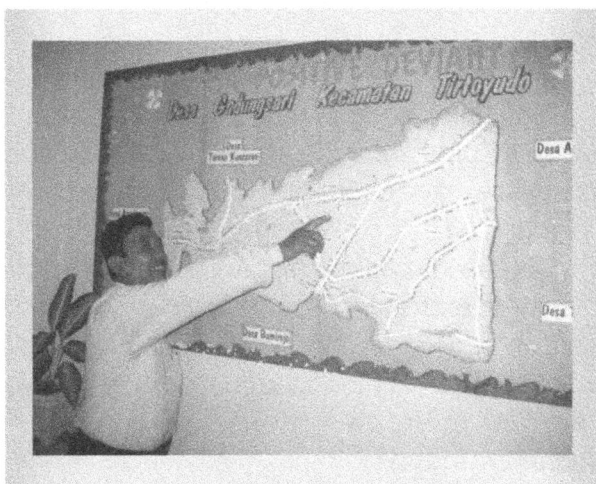

The PD map is hung on the wall of Pak Kasmadi's home
as a permanent fixture

"The PD mapping exercise was like playing with a puzzle and making sense of the big picture."[36] From that point on, kaders and community members began to take ownership of the "silent" problem of missing girls, posing questions such as, "Why do girls leave the village, why not boys?" Realizing that although an answer like, "They make money more easily," was a simple one, they probed further: "But why? Where do they work?" And further: "At a bar. What is a bar for you? A discotheque? Or perhaps a place where sex is bought and sold?" Through the detailed house-by-house, street-by-street, village level mapping, the community was able to identify the specific issues faced by the population of vulnerable girls.

35 In the conference call with Titing Martini (see footnote) we asked her to tell us what was salient for her about the mapping activity.
36 Titing Martini, Conference call with authors, September 8, 2008.

PD Selection Criteria

After the mapping activity, the Gadungsari community identified the criteria for selecting the PD girls, those who did not succumb to trafficking, and PD families, those who did not send their girls into the sex industry.[37]

The PD selection criteria for a girl were two: (1) she had to be poor[38] and be under 18 years old, and (2) she must have made a conscious decision not to work in the sex industry, despite the opportunity to do so. To be considered a PD, a family had to be poor, have at least three children with at least one daughter who was 15+ years old and no longer in school, and parents who had no more than a junior high school education and would not permit their daughter(s) to work in the entertainment industry.

In implementing the PD project in Gadungsari, the community decided to focus especially on the behavioral practices of PD families, given the PD girls were subsets of PD families, and parents played an influential role in deciding whether or not a girl would travel outside the village for work.

Practices of PD Families[39]

You need to let go of the head but hold on to the tail.—*Pak Darma*

Pak Darma is a farmer who expressed publicly

---

37 LPKP Jawa Timur, Save the Children in Indonesia. The Positive Deviance Approach for preventing girl trafficking.
 http://www.positivedeviance.org/projects/indgirltraffick/
38 That is, work as farmers or seasonal laborers.
39 LPKP Jawa Timur, Save the Children in Indonesia. The Positive Deviance Approach for preventing girl trafficking.
http://www.positivedeviance.org/projects/indgirltraffick/

his opposition to allowing girls to work in the entertainment industry. By "letting go of the head but holding on to the tail," Pak Darma meant that as a parent one should permit a degree of autonomy to the child without relinquishing responsibility for what the children are doing.[40] By interviewing families like Pak Darma's and others, the community identified several PD strategies and practices that helped families to reduce their vulnerability for girl trafficking, including

> Engaging in a variety of income-generating activities, including growing a diverse array of crops (e.g. rice, coffee, corn, vanilla beans), raising poultry and livestock, establishing fish farms and others.
> Helping their daughters to establish a small business to supplement family income.
> Openly discussing with their children the risks of working in the "entertainment industry" and supporting the scoping of other alternatives.
> Emphasizing the value of both formal and vocational education for their daughters.
> Allowing their daughters to work outside the village, after closely investigating the employer, and the kind of work she will be doing.
> Requiring their daughters to report home regularly via letters and phone if indeed they do take employment outside the village.

Design and Implementation[41]

Once PD practices followed by families such as Pak Darma's were identified, a community meeting was

---

40 Interview with Pak Darma, a PD father, can be found on the Positive Deviance website: http://www.positivedeviance.org/projects/indgirltraffick/
41 LPKP Jawa Timur, Save the Children Indonesia. The Positive Deviance Approach for preventing girl trafficking.
http://www.positivedeviance.org/projects/indgirltraffick/

held in Gadungsari to share the PD inquiry results and build consensus on how to act on these practices. Through several rounds of deliberations and iterations, supported by kaders, representatives of the LPKP, and Pak Kasmadi, the community agreed on and initiated their own action plan to combat trafficking. Community watch committees consisting of kaders, PD families, formal and informal leaders, and other villagers were established in every hamlet to monitor the brokers and traffickers and to map the migration flow of girls. Volunteers approached families who were thought to be at risk for trafficking to discuss the risks of working in the entertainment industry, and how to make migration safer.

The community also launched an anti-trafficking campaign, which included enlisting families to spread messages and act as role models. These messages were developed based on PD practices and experiences to promote a fundamental shift in values with respect to trafficking. An extensive agriculture training program involving crop rotation practices, planting of cash crops, and marketing and distributing value-added agricultural products (e.g., banana chips) was hatched. Community leaders also worked with local government officials to develop economic opportunities for women and girls and to adopt standards with respect to a travel documentation, employment verification and regular reporting.

The local government disseminated rules and regulations regarding the travel documentation needed to all hamlet leaders to distribute to their community members. Girls of ages 14 to 16 in Gadungsari were specifically targeted with information about the risks of leaving the village to work in "unclear" destinations. And they discussed sex trade issues with other neighboring villages and the sub-district government officials.

PD Progress in Gadungsari Village

In 2005, two years after the PD project got under way in Gadungsari, village *kaders*, LPKP staff and Save the Children representatives, noted the following accomplishments of the PD pilot program:[42]

1. **No new girls had left Gadungsari to enter the sex trade** (massage parlors, brothels, etc.) since the beginning of the PD anti-trafficking program.

2. **Twenty averted attempts at girl trafficking were documented.**[43]

3. **The use of travel papers was rigorously enforced.**[44]

4. **The community "watch group"**[45] **was actively involved in** identifying high-risk girls and visited their families for counseling. They also closely monitored the veracity of information furnished in travel documents, identifying red flags that might suggest trafficking.

---

42 Positive Deviance Initiative/Save the Children (2005). Two years after the workshop - Gadung Sari village
.http://www.positivedeviance.org/projects/indgirltraffick/updateApr2006.html
43 "Averted" is defined in this document as a high-risk girl, i.e. between the age of 15-18 and not in school, who had been approached by the broker, or who had filled out travel papers to leave the community for "unknown employment," who was persuaded not to leave.
44 Travel papers required anyone planning to leave the village to indicate their new address and purpose of work.
45 The Community Watch Group was composed of 15 members, one from each hamlet.

81

5.   **A Girls Forum (club) was created in Gadungsari** providing an opportunity for village girls to have a designated place to meet, discuss issues of mutual interest, provide tutoring for younger girls, and enjoy activities such as reading, painting and sewing.[46]

6.   **The village received a commitment from the district government** for funds to expand training opportunities for girls in the village. Also, village leaders met with officials of the Ministry of National Education at the district level to include trafficking/health risk issues in the school curriculum.

7.   **The taboo on talking about trafficking was broken** as evidenced through anti-trafficking messages routinely delivered in the mosque, in Koran reading sessions, and in schools. Community members in Gadungsari now openly talked about the dangers and risks associated with trafficking.

8.   **The community held a poster contest** for which each hamlet in Gadungsari submitted two posters. Of the 30 posters submitted by the 15 hamlets in Gadungsari, three were chosen to be reproduced in calendar-form. Some 2,000 anti-trafficking calendars were printed and distributed to each household in the community and to district and provincial government offices. The contests and the

---

[46] The girls youth club is located in a house donated by a local citizen and is open four days a week. A village volunteer is present at the center every day to address questions including those related to risks of "leaving the village." The center also provides girls with the opportunity to tutor younger girls in reading and math, thus enhancing their own self-esteem and feelings of "having an important role to play in the community."

calendars kept the buzz going on anti-trafficking.

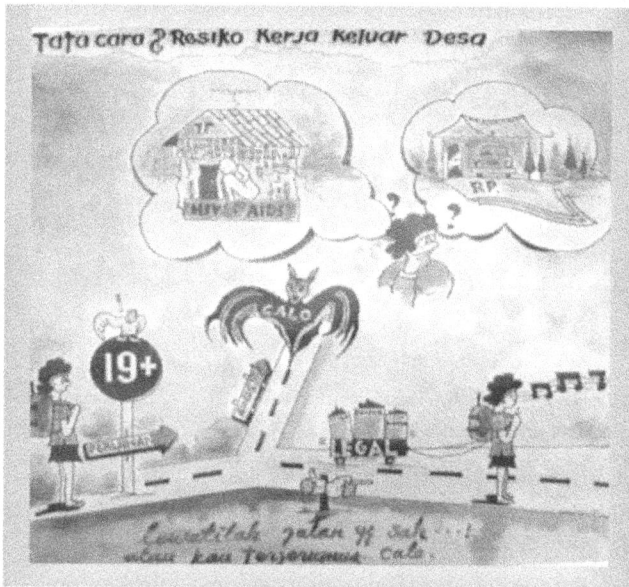

Photograph of a winning anti-trafficking poster later reproduced in calendar form and distributed widely[47]

Expansion of Anti-Trafficking Programs in East Java

One of the most evident causes for the success of the pilot project in Gadungsari, apart from the dedication and time investment of community volunteers, village *kaders*, as well as LPKP and Save the Children facilitators was that this program was community owned and run. Building on the momentum generated by the PD project in Gadungsari and in other pilot villages, in 2005, Save the Children facilitated government and civil society partnerships to develop a provincial plan of action (RAP) in East Java against child trafficking, aligning it with Indonesia's national plan of action on trafficking. The RAP identifies

---

47 Poster image taken from background document provided by Save the Children Staff: Brief information on Save the Children-IFO trafficking prevention program.

priorities for the development of provincial policy and provides grants to local NGOs to support follow up implementation.   In March 2005, the provincial secretary in East Java signed the action plan and adopted it as a provincial regulation. In May 2005, the *Bupatis* (District Regents) in the Malang and Tulungagung Districts of East Java signed district-level action plans to combat trafficking.[48]

ENABLE and ENACT

In September 2004, the success of the PD program in Gadungsari and in other pilot sites in East Java encouraged Save the Children to partner with the International Organization of Migration (IOM), to launch a four-and-a-half year, scaled-up program on girl trafficking called ENABLE (Enabling Communities to Combat Child Trafficking through Education) in Indonesia with funding from the U.S. Department of Labor.

ENABLE was designed to encourage community ownership and sustainability of the anti-trafficking program, and as a result Save the Children established close partnerships with government structures, local faith-based organizations and local *kaders* to ensure its longevity.   In each ENABLE site, Save the Children established village education committees (*Komite Pendidikan Masyarakat Desa*, or KPMD), drawing upon respected, can-do local *kaders*.

Targeted at 100 communities and 19,500 at-risk children and young beneficiaries in five districts of East Java, ENABLE's purpose was to improve access and quality of formal and non-formal education using an

---

48 Save the Children—IFO. Brief information on Save the Children-IFO trafficking prevention program (2005). Provided by Save the Children as background information.

intervention model called Enabling Community Action (ENACT).[49] Under ENACT, villages engaged in trafficking (referred to as "sending" villages) and/or at high risk of becoming so were "supported to map and mobilize community resources, strengthen local commitment to keep children in school and out of exploitative labor, and advocate to bring more government attention of the most vulnerable children."[50] Of these 100 communities, 23 communities, where the population migration rate was over 30 percent and which were identified as being "sending" villages, were selected to employ the deeper and more labor- and time-intensive positive deviance approach to reduce girl trafficking.

Results from the field suggested that by the end of the first year of implementation, the PD villages within ENABLE had met their objective to build the capacity of a local NGO partner and community volunteers to apply the PD approach and design an actionable intervention. The outcomes at the end of the first year in the 23 villages were similar to some of the outcomes experienced in Gadungsari:[51]

1.   **The number of girls trafficked in the PD intervention villages was reduced to zero.**

---

49 Refer to Save the Children (2006, January 20). Final Project Document under USDOL and Save the Children, Inc. Cooperative Agreement. Washington D.C.: Save the Children. The ENACT model draws on a social systems approach to individual and social change, and builds on Save the Children's previous experiences in promoting social change through a Community Action Cycle (CAC). The principles of ENACT include: involving the individuals most affected; being biased towards local content and ownership; supporting dialogue and debate on issues that resonate with the community; and ensuring that communities are the agents of their own change. Within Indonesia's Urban Street Children program, the ENACT model had been used to successfully map and mobilize community resources, strengthen community commitment to keep children off the street, and advocate to bring more government attention to needs of the most vulnerable children.
50 Save the Children. Final Project Document Under USDOL and Save the Children, Inc. Cooperative Agreement. Washington, DC: Save the Children, January 20, 2006.
51 Save the Children-IFO. Grassroots anti-trafficking: annual, end of grant report (2005). Provided as background information.

2.   **Each village developed rules to regulate the legal movement of people**, especially of children and girls.

3.   **Each village established community watch groups** to monitor movement of girls and brokers in and to their villages.

4.   **A network of formal village leaders was established** to raise awareness of other village leaders; the network actively participates in district government meetings to discuss the issue of trafficking.

5.   **Three villages worked with local police** to document cases of trafficking and brought one broker to court.

6.   **Approximately 5,000 families (20,000 individuals) indirectly benefitted** from the project during the first year.

To gain a better understanding of the multilayered PD process as it played out over different lengths of time, our 2008 qualitative assessment of the PD approach to reduce girl trafficking in Indonesia centers on two communities in East Java:

1.   Village Gadungsari in District Malang where Save the Children piloted the PD approach beginning in mid-2003 with Oak Foundation support, and

2.   Village Kedoyo in District Tulungagung where Save the Children launched the PD

approach in April 2007 as part of the ENABLE project with support from the U.S. Department of Labor.

First, we discuss our qualitative findings from Village Gadungsari, followed by findings from Village Kedoyo.

PD Practices in Gadungsari: From Pilot to Ever-Expanding Ripples

The village *kaders* and parents in Village Gadungsari, many of whom had been actively involved in implementing the PD program since its inception in 2003, identified several PD practices that they believed had made a significant difference in reducing the trafficking of young girls. The adoption of any one PD practice in Gadungsari by itself could perhaps only do so much, but taken together, and over a five-year time period, they had significantly improved the quality of life of its residents. Clearly, the PD work had moved beyond being a pilot project focusing initially on girl trafficking to becoming a mainstreamed approach in other village development sectors. As a village *kader* emphasized, "Gadungsari has adopted PD as its development premise and mantra."

Expanded Parental Communication, Schooling, and Income-Generation

Uttari's sketch illustrated the various PD practices that have reduced girl trafficking in Gadungsari.

Uttari's sketch describing the PD practices that have
been adopted in Gadungsari to reduce girl trafficking

Uttari explained:

First, you see a child [holding a doll] with parents.
Open communication between parents and
children is important. So, one PD practice is parents
loving and caring for their children. Second, you see
a girl who has continued in school [pointing to her
uniform] and earned a minimum of secondary
education. Third, you see different types of
income-generating activities. PD families have
different sources of income. Here they are raising
poultry and engaged in growing different crops.
Fourth, education can lead to new knowledge and
skills and a better future. And, fifth, this knowledge
can be shared with others in one's group to help
everyone.

Yuda, another *kader* member, drew the
following sketch to outline the sequential progression
[shown by arrows] of how these PD practices interrelate
and feed into one another.

Yuda's sketch depicting the cumulative effect of adopting a wide variety of PD practices, which have led to reducing girl trafficking in Gadungsari

Yuda narrated:

The first image is of parents in the field receiving help from their children and giving them back a cut of the money earned for their work. The children can buy things for themselves and can save money in the *kendi* (saving basket). Then you see girls who now continue their education until senior high school. In my sketch, I show parents [sitting at the head of the table] keeping an eye on their children and talking to them about career options and the importance of making good choices. The parents suggest learning marketable skills like sewing [top right], making plastic flowers, and then selling them in open spaces [points to a girl displaying her flowers on a table while clutching money in her hand]. Other groups make sandals and sell them in the market to make money. Another PD practice in Gadungsari is the discussion of these issues in religious meetings. Finally, in Gadundsari, now people openly talk about the ills of trafficking, including HIV. Now, girls and their families know that trafficking is dangerous and there are alternatives to going outside.

Yuda's narration, which was met by nods and a big round of applause from other *kaders* and parents, reinforces the value of parental involvement and guidance in children's career decisions. It emphasizes that although many children contributed to the family income, they were still materially and emotionally dependent on their parents. The importance of close parental relationships and interdependence was further amplified by Citra's sketch and narration.

Citra's aspirations to be a dress designer
with the help of her father

Citra, an 18-year-old girl, who is a *kader* member in one of Gadungsari's youth organizations, explained:

The picture shows the expectations that my parents and I have for my future. At this time, I go to vocational school. I also want to complete senior high school. Then I intend to get training in sewing and dress designing. Then I can ask my friends who can't continue their studies in Gadungsari to work with me. I see my life as a career woman, a dress designer. I will establish a designer's company and make clothes with my friends. I have a strategy to achieve this—my father is a tailor so I will learn and continue to run his shop.

Citra, who privately acknowledged that she would have been at-risk for trafficking if the PD program had not come to Gadungsari, emphasized the value of both formal and informal schooling as two key PD practices that most families in her village had adopted, including her own. As a youth *kader* member, she was mindful about finding employment opportunities for other youth in Gadungsari. And she believed that her plan to become a dress designer was feasible because her father was a tailor, and would support and train her as an apprentice. Thus, through Citra's account we see the value of close parental involvement in shaping a young person's future.

As one would expect, Uttari, Yuda, and Citra's rendition of PD practices that families in Gadungsari had adopted to reduce girl trafficking are closely aligned with the list of PD behaviors identified during the community-led PD inquiry, conducted in Gadungsari some four-and-a-half years previously. We found that these previously identified PD behaviors, and certain new ones, that community members identified over time, repeated themselves with regularity in our respondents' sketches and narrations.

Pak Kasmadi, Gadungsari's village secretary and a champion of the PD initiative from its inception, highlighted several "new" positive deviant practices that the community members had identified and adopted in their quest to reduce girl trafficking, and which had spilled over to other village-development activities. He noted, "Several small but important PD practices that have emerged in Gadungsari over time have made a big difference."

Walking With, Watching Over, and Talking More with Children

Pak Kasmadi went on to say, "Many parents now try to accompany their children to school and walk back with them. It reinforces the value they place on education. Also the children feel supported by this very personal involvement." He added, "There is a village watch committee in Gadungsari which keeps a close eye on the girls who leave the village. They work closely with the village office ensuring they have proper identification cards, job employment certificate and responsible employers." And, he said, "Many parents now buy mobile telephone credit vouchers for their girls who work outside, so that the girls can call them at any time, and they can be in regular touch with their girls. Some members of the village watch committee also call the girls."

Connecting Ideas with Resources

Pak Kasmadi was most enthusiastic about the payoffs accruing from the PD practice of increased interaction between the leaders and community members of Gadungsari and the local district officials. He emphasized:

When we thought about starting income-generating activities for young girls, we realized several resources were available from the district and provincial government. We began to interact more closely with district officials, asking for advice and support. Many of them came to visit Gadungsari and began taking interest. The relationships we developed, and the trust we built, led to micro-loans for young girls to invest in a small businesses, and helped village women obtain sewing machines, kitchen equipment and large-fryers for making ginger, banana and cassava chips. Further, our increased interactions with local government officials have helped make Desa Gadungsari a 'model' village.

PD Mainstreaming in Gadungsari's Development Plans

Pak Kasmadi made another important point: "PD practices are now completely mainstreamed in all of Gadungsari's cross-sectoral development programs, whether reduction in trafficking, income-generation and livelihoods, formal and non-formal education, agricultural practices, credit and loan programs and others." To illustrate, Pak Kasmadi pulled out a detailed poster-like schema, created in his neat handwriting with dozens of boxes, circles and arrows, showing the integration of PD practices in Gadungsari's overall development plan. He emphasized that the plan resulted from numerous citizen meetings in Gadungsari, as well as interactions with district and provincial officials, and thus matched the needs of villagers with state-supported resources and structures.

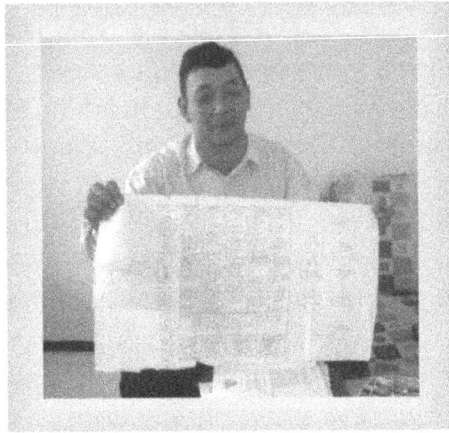

Pak Kasmadi emphasizing the centrality of PD practices inGadungsari's development planning

Pak Kasmadi emphasized, "In January, 2008, 11 women in Gadungsari received kitchen equipment and large fryers to engage in business ventures to make chips." He continued, "Here [in the photo] you see the government official from the Department of Women's Empowerment in Malang District handing over the equipment in an official ceremony while another recipient looks on. Each of the 11 women who received the equipment will hire anywhere from three to 10 women or young girls in this venture. So, this means employment for 50 to 60 residents of Gadungsari, who may have traveled outside for jobs."

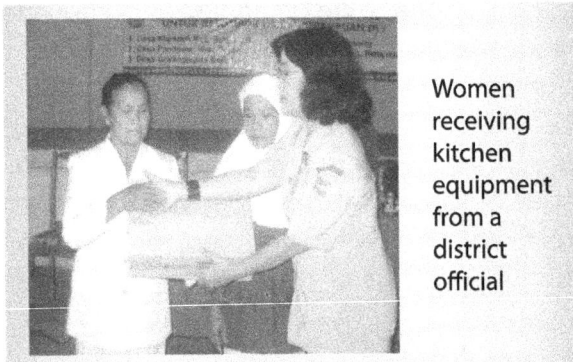

Women receiving kitchen equipment from a district official

We visited a small one-room factory (about 12 feet by 14 feet in size) that specialized in making sweet ginger chips. It employed 15 women and produced 180 one kilogram bags of chips a day. All the bags were sold to one buyer at the unit price of Rp. 15,000 ($1.60), who then distributed among many shopkeepers in neighboring villages and towns. The average daily pay for young women employed here was Rp. 12,000 ($1.25), a decent and honorable wage by rural Indonesian standards.

Young girls at work in a business which produces ginger chips

Right next to the ginger-chip factory were several enterprises making banana and cassava chips. Rows of raised platforms lined the street where tens of thousands of cassava and banana chips lay for drying.

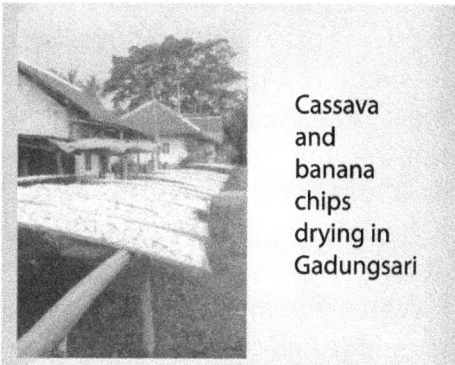

Cassava and banana chips drying in Gadungsari

Lestari's sketch and narration also emphasized how, over the past few years, the kaders and village leaders in Gadungsari had tapped government resources to support entrepreneurial business ventures.

Lestari's banana chips venture

Lestari noted:

I wanted to do my own business. I observed there are many banana trees in my village. So, I thought we can make a business out of them. I picked some bananas and experimented with making banana chips. I gave them to my neighbors to taste and many of them said they were delicious. So, I started this business venture and taught several others how to make them. Initially, my neighbor helped me to sell them in the market. Then, one day I met an entrepreneur and asked for his advice on how to distribute the chips even more widely. I also met with Pak Kasmadi and other village leaders to get support to match my capital and help my company grow. They suggested that we make a proposal to the district government office. We made the proposal and we got support for this venture from the district women empowerment fund and purchased equipment to make even more banana chips. We also borrowed capital at a low interest. Then my friends and I started distributing these chips at supermarkets. Now I make a decent profit, employ several people and am saving for my family.

We asked Lestari how, in her opinion, the PD program had been a source of motivation for her banana chips business, and she explained, "PD tells you that solutions lie in one's own environment. So I looked for how to make a business harnessing what exists in my village. Then the banana trees began to speak to me." With support from village leaders, Lestari was able to connect her business ideas with an external network of resources, establishing links to credit, technical advice and markets. Today, Lestari mentors other young girls to tap business opportunities in the local environment.

In summary, the adoption of PD practices in Gadungsari to reduce child trafficking have, over time, rippled across other village development initiatives, leading to the adoption of other innovative business and social practices. As one of the kader members noted, "PD has become so mainstreamed in Gadungsari that one routinely comes across families who are not even at risk for girl trafficking for they have no girls, but who access loans, grow vanilla beans, raise livestock and are engaged in making chips."

Positive Changes in Gadungsari

Our respondents in Gadungsari—parents,

kaders, and village development officials—reflected on how the PD program had brought positive changes in the community. Upon our arrival in Gadungsari, Pak Kasmadi apologized for not being able to arrange for us to talk to girls who might have been "at risk" for trafficking before the PD program was initiated [we had expressed a desire beforehand to talk to girls in their mid-to late teens]. He noted, "Almost all teenage girls in Gadungsari are in junior or senior secondary school, or enrolled in vocational classes." Our inability to meet teenage girls in Gadungsari was, ironically, a result of the effectiveness of the PD program.

Yuda and Sinta, two highly active *kader* members, reflected on the changes in Gadungsari since the PD program was launched in mid-2003. Their sketch and narration helped set the "before" and "after" scene in Gadungsari.

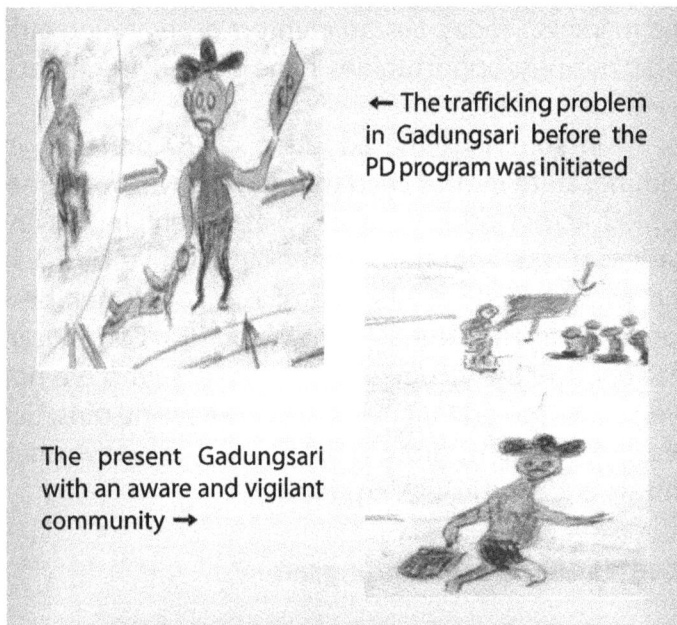

← The trafficking problem in Gadungsari before the PD program was initiated

The present Gadungsari with an aware and vigilant community →

Yuda narrated, "Before the PD program was initiated in Gadungsari, traffickers came into the village to recruit girls in a very subtle way. They lent them money to help their poor parents, so the parents were in debt bondage. The girls were taken out of the community without government identification papers so they were hard to track."

Then pointing to another sketch, Yuda narrated the "after" status of girl trafficking in Gadungsari: "After PD came, we understood the importance of ID cards. We worked with regional government and local officials to make posters and educate the community about how to work outside the community legally. The traffickers became frustrated and left." Then, he added, "In early 2004, when we conducted the PD inquiry and community mapping, we identified 33 'missing' girls. They were all working in the entertainment/sex industry. In 2008, it is only six girls; they come from very poor families, and they also are trying to equip themselves with other skills so that they can change jobs."

The poor socioeconomic conditions that families found themselves in five years ago were a common thread echoed by our respondents. As one parent noted:

Before PD came to Gadungsari, it was a 'sleepy' village. There was gambling, youth did not have a bright future, families placed low value on educating girls, and there was very poor infrastructure—no roads or piped water supply. Our community could not develop because we did not have updated knowledge about agricultural practices, and we had little communication with government officials and other sources of support. Now it has 'woken' up. Today, children in Gadungsari attend kindergarten, elementary school and junior high school. And they can go to senior high school or to vocational school. They can grow crops that fetch good money like vanilla, ginger, and cassava. They have learned business skills and can add value to the products by making banana or cassava chips and selling them in the market.

Uttari and Nirmala's [both *kaders*] "before" and "after" sketches were also revealing in highlighting the changes in Gadungsari before and after the initiation of the PD initiative in 2003.

Uttari and Nirmala's "before" sketch of Gadungsari

Uttari narrated, "Before PD came, only the traditional methods for cultivation were used, few marketable goods were produced, distribution was limited, and girls and women worked in entertainment bars. We overheard some had even fallen sick and died of incurable diseases. People were poor, and several girls would go abroad [outside the village]. Many women were exploited, and many children were neglected."

Uttari's and Nirmala's "after" sketch (below) tells a different story—one of a transformed Gadungsari

Uttari and Nirmala's "after" sketch of Gadungsari

Uttari narrated:

Today the agricultural practices have changed. We are planting different crops. We are turning them into marketable products like cassava and banana chips. People are also raising chickens, goats, and cows. If someone wants to work abroad [outside the village], they can get the documents to do it legally and there are programs to assist them in getting a decent job. Today, the parents look after their children, and the government looks after its citizens.

Pak Kasmadi added:

The village is more organized now. There are more village-based organizations, and there is better coordination among them and between them and outside agencies. Leaders, *kaders* and citizens gather routinely to discuss activities and self-help projects. For instance, community members decided to double the diameter of the seven-kilometer pipe that distributes water to homes in Gadungsari so that everyone's water requirements could be adequately and fairly met. Citizens made a 'gentleman's rule:' ...those whose houses are in higher elevations must use water carefully or those who live below will have no water.

Pak Kasmadi also believed that, relative to other communities, Gadungsari, thanks to its brush with the positive deviance approach, was more socially cohesive, as characterized by high levels of trust between its citizens, neighborly reciprocity and a high degree of volunteerism. In essence, Gadungsari had become a community where a lot of "capital" was vested in social relationships, which led to greater common good.

In summary, the "before" and "after" sketches and narrations provide a general sense of the changes participants from the Gadungsari community perceived. We see that many of the positive changes center on using different methods for cultivation, an expanded portfolio of income-generating activities, formal and non-formal education, and open lines of communication at various levels (for instance, between parents and children, among neighbors, and between village leaders and government officials).

The adoption of PD practices in Gadungsari had, undoubtedly, improved the quality of life of its residents. Over time, the PD project had moved beyond the pilot stage focused on the single issue of girl trafficking to become a mainstreamed development activity, integrated with other cross-sectoral programs in education, income-generation and livelihoods, nutrition, and physical and psychological health.

Next, let's see what PD practices to reduce girl trafficking were identified and adopted in Desa Kedoyo in District Tulungugung, a village known to send out its girls to work in the sex industry, where Save the Children began PD implementation in April 2007.

PD Practices Adopted by Families in Kedoyo

The village *kaders* and parents, many of whom had been actively involved in implementing the PD program in the past 16 months, identified several PD practices that they believed had made a significant difference in reducing the trafficking of young girls. In contrast to Gadungsari, where the PD pilot project on reducing girl trafficking initiated five years previously seemed, in 2008, to be seamlessly integrated into its fabric of development programs, the program in Kedoyo was relatively young but showed palpable evidence of effectiveness.

Saving More, Studying More, Learning More and Working More

Haryono, a *kader* member, drew a sketch to illustrate the various PD practices that families had adopted that had helped in reducing girl trafficking in Kedoyo.

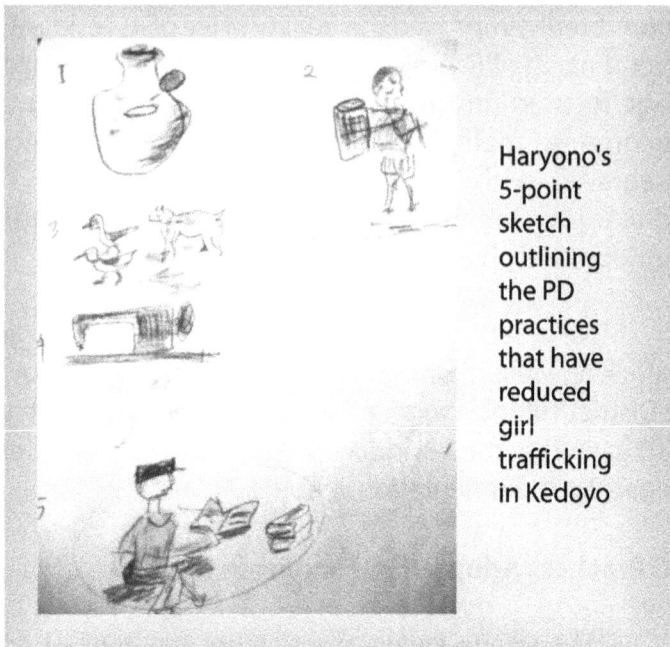

Haryono's 5-point sketch outlining the PD practices that have reduced girl trafficking in Kedoyo

Pointing to his five-point sketch, Haryono explained:

First, members of most families in Kedoyo including mother, father, boys and girls have become very mindful about saving money. Even small coins are put in the *kendi*, a basket with an opening on the side [akin to a piggy bank]. This saved money can be used for small business ventures like preparing snacks for selling in the market, to buy books or to buy school uniforms. Second, after children return from school, the girls, especially, now spend time in the agricultural field, helping their mothers. Some even work in other people's fields and earn extra money. Third, families in Kedoyo now have many more income-generating options besides farming. Many families breed livestock – chicken, goats and cows. The eggs, milk and meat are consumed in homes, which results in better nutrition, and the extra is sold in the market to earn cash income. Fourth, many young girls now have the opportunity to enroll in sewing classes or to run a beauty salon. Many learn to do embroidery. They get jobs easily in Malang or other towns in textile factories. Fifth, most of the children in Kedoyo, including teenage girls, attend school or some other form of non-formal, vocational education. After school, they work harder in the fields as well as study harder at home. They will necessarily have a brighter future when they graduate....definitely, a lot brighter than young girls in Kedoyo a few years ago, who now work outside.

The culture of saving as a PD practice was emphasized in several other sketches. Rasha, a parent of two teenage girls drew the following sketch and noted, "When one saves, one is not saving just money. One is saving the future of one's children. One is investing in ensuring they have decent and honorable lives. I have realized how important it is for us to save, even if it is a few coins each day." Pointing to her sketch in which the *kendi*, the savings basket, is drawn taller than her daughter for symbolic purposes, Rasha said emphatically, "Savings equals a bright future for our girls."

Rasha's sketch of a *kendi* depicting savings equals a bright future for girls

The sketches that follow, drawn by "at-risk-for-trafficking" teenage girls in Kedoyo, also elaborate on the PD practices that have been adopted by several families. Participating in educational and income-generating activities emerged repeatedly as key PD practices. Intan and Wulan, two 14-year-old girls in Kedoyo, drew the following four-sided sketch, and explained, "It is important to stay in school. Although our family is poor, we have the motivation and confidence and commitment to continue our studies."

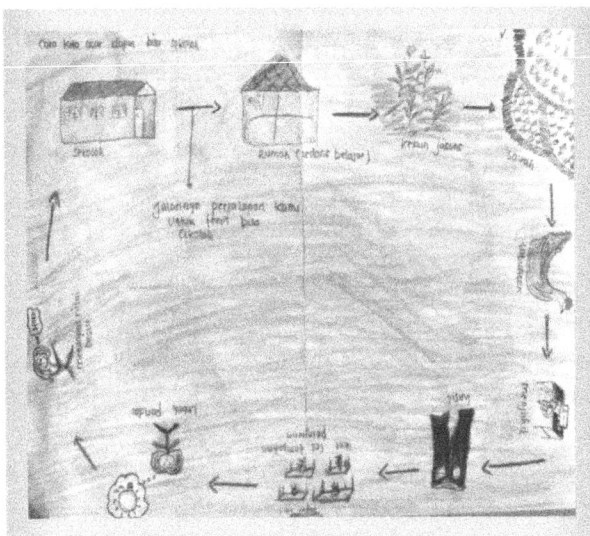

Intan and Wulan's sketch showing school, studying, developing vocational skills, earning and saving

Pointing to the lower left portion of their sketch, Intan explained, "You can see we study at home." Then pointing to the upper right portion of their sketch, she and Wulan continued, "We are growing corn and helping our parents in the field. We are saving and taking sewing courses. We take other courses to become educated. We are acquiring knowledge and skills and getting smarter."

106

Similarly, Ratu and Eka stated that, for them, the first key practice to adopt was to have conviction in one's heart. When asked where their conviction came from, they responded that it was from seeing other girls find success.

Ratu and Eka's sketch emphasizing the importance of acquiring skills such as running a beauty salon or sewing, which can yield income and savings

Ratu explained:

The first practice is to have conviction in your heart. Second, we participated in a beauty salon course [pointing to the red cheeks with rouge]. We also went to attend a government-supported sewing course in Blitar, a neighboring town. After six months in Blitar, we were provided with a sewing machine, and if we are still sewing after a year we will get another machine to expand our business and to train someone else. By doing embroidery we can earn money. And save some.

Other girls in Kedoyo had found ways to earn a junior or senior secondary equivalence certificate while generating income from growing and selling flowers, sewing, or working in their neighbor's house, as Bethari and Bethari depicted in their sketch.

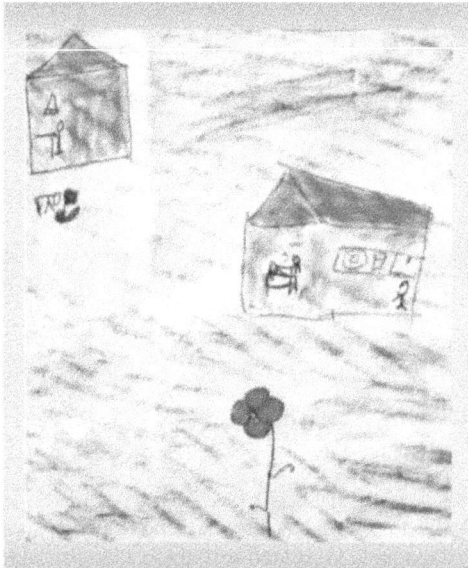

Bethari's multiple income-generating activities: sewing, growing flowers and helping neighbor with household chores

Bethari narrated, "We take the senior high school equivalency and study at home. We are growing flowers and plants to sell, and we are also taking sewing and embroidery courses." Pointing to the house on the right, Bethari continued, "We also help our neighbors with dishwashing to make some money. We spend money carefully to buy food and clothes. An agent comes to collect the plants, and he asks us if we can grow more."

Looking at the sketches of Haryono, Rasha, Intan, Ratu and Bethari, and hearing their narrations on the PD practices that were identified and adopted by families in Kedoyo to reduce the incidence of girl trafficking, we see the overlap that exists between PD behaviors identified in Gadungsari and then independently several years later in Kedoyo. In both locations, we see that PD families emphasized the value of both formal and vocational education for their daughters; supported their daughters to establish a business venture; engaged in a variety of income-generating activities, including agricultural production, raising livestock and growing flowers; consciously saved money; and found ways to connect their needs and aspirations with existing programs that were state-supported or state-sponsored.

The availability of vocational training and local employment opportunities, as well as enhanced incomes and personal savings, had contributed greatly to raising the material and social capital of Kedoyo. The kaders and community leaders in Kedoyo privately told us about five women in Kedoyo who previously worked in the sex industry but now were back making a living in Kedoyo. We were introduced to one of them, who noted that, "A year into the project, Kedoyo is experiencing significant, deep-rooted changes in attitudes and behaviors."

Visible Signs of Change in Kedoyo

The ability of boys and girls in Kedoyo to obtain an education, both formal and informal, and enroll in various vocational courses (sewing, flower growing, motorcycle repair and others) was the visible sign of change most noted by our respondents after the PD program arrived in Kedoyo. In their sketches and narrations, the "at-risk" girls, their parents, and village kaders enthusiastically hailed the availability of junior and senior high school equivalency programs because now it meant that young girls and boys could now work in Kedoyo, help with household chores and not have to drop out of school.

Expanded Learning Opportunities

Our respondents emphasized that seeing other boys and girls engaged in both educational and income-generating activities was inspirational to others because peer-based role modeling works especially well with young people. No one wanted to be left behind. In their sketches, we saw numerous references to various types of vocational courses that provided opportunities for generating income, and the possibility of making a decent living either in Kedoyo, or a neighboring town.

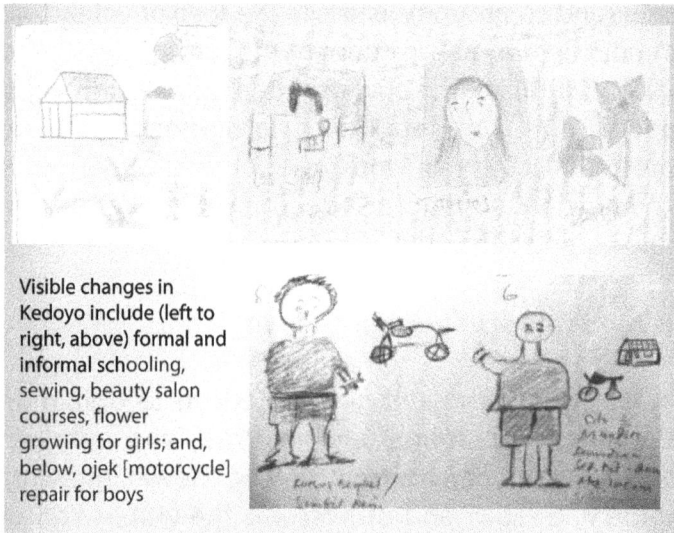

Visible changes in Kedoyo include (left to right, above) formal and informal schooling, sewing, beauty salon courses, flower growing for girls; and, below, ojek [motorcycle] repair for boys

More Conversations

Another sign of change in Kedoyo cited by many of our respondents was the rise in the numbers of group meetings, *kader* discussions, citizen forums, and interactions of community members with district level government officials.

As the following sketch and narration by two *kader* members illustrates, "Meetings now occur in Kedoyo in mosques, village offices and neighborhoods, covering a variety of topics from expanding educational opportunities, to infrastructure development, to expanding the range of vocational courses and income-generating activities."

More dialogue, debate and discussion
is now visible in Kedoyo

In closing, the village chairperson summarized the influence of the PD program in Kedoyo as follows: "Since PD came to Kedoyo, it seems the village is coming together to discuss and solve its problems. The kader now are more vigilant, alert and motivated, and the parents see a brighter future for their children and themselves."

A village elder, who was silent for most of the day, added, "The sun is just rising in Kedoyo. There are more people involved in more activities. There is more energy. This bodes well for the village's future. Come back and see us in a few years."

In Conclusion

In conclusion, what can we deduce from our qualitative findings from Gadungsari and Kedoyo?

While the PD project did not put a stop to girl trafficking altogether, it did prevent several of them from being recruited in the project sites.

The sketches and narrations from Gadungsari show the evolution of a culture of investment in both local livelihoods and people. In the five years since the PD program was launched, the quality of life of Gadungsari's residents had markedly improved. The PD approach in Gadungsari had moved beyond girl trafficking to become an integral part of other village-based development activities in education, income-generation and livelihoods, and physical and social health.

A year into the project, Kedoyo exhibited positive signs of change. The sketches and narrations from Kedoyo show that families were highly invested in the reduction of girl trafficking in their community.

The PD experiences in Gadungsari and Kedoyo point to at least two crucial elements in consolidating and expanding PD: (1) community ownership of the PD inquiry (PDI), the sense-making of its findings, and designing and implementing an actionable plan based on the PDI for amplification; and (2) formation and maintenance of strong relationships with partner NGOs and government officials at the local and regional levels. We see through the Gadungsari and Kedoyo experiences that when these relationships begin early, and all stakeholders are involved in the project planning stages as well as in the PDI, success and sustainability are more likely to be attained.

Part 6
Conclusions, Lessons and Recommendations for Using Positive Deviance for Child Protection

PD questions the assumption that beneficiaries are helpless....that they know nothing and can do nothing without outside help. My experience in northern Uganda tells me that the beneficiaries are the real actors. They drive the PD wagon. At best, Save the Children staff members help them to access some fuel.[52]

This monograph analyzes two positive deviance projects focusing on child protection issues in Uganda and Indonesia. Our analysis was based on (1) a review of the available archival documentation on both projects, and (2) in-depth interviews and participatory data-collection activities with project implementers, positive deviants and community members in both locations.

In this concluding part, organized in three sub-sections, we (1) distill what the PD implementers in Uganda and Indonesia believed to be the key attributes of the PD strategy, (2) explicate the lessons learned about PD as a community-centered approach to social change, including its relevance and usefulness for child protection issues and implications for scalability and sustainability, and (3) make certain recommendations about harnessing and strengthening the investments made in pioneering the PD approach for child protection.

---

52 Paska Aber, PD Project Coordinator, Save the Children. Interview with author, Uganda Pader District, 2008.

First, some caveats and author notes are in order.

In making sense of our field-based experiences and in crafting this concluding section, we have purposely tried to adhere to certain key principles that are fundamental to the positive deviance approach: that is, the wisdom lies with the various actors involved in the community of PD practice, and those in the trenches in Uganda and Indonesia know best what works (or does not work). So, to ascertain the key lessons learned about PD as a social change strategy, and to provide recommendations about strengthening PD within Save the Children, we have tried to "listen" carefully to what our key informants and respondents shared with us during our field visits and/or through the available archival materials. As previously noted, our sense-making process involved in-depth reading and analysis of field notes[53] through several iterations, and repeated reviews of our 223 sketches and narrations provided by our 121 respondents, looking for thematic patterns and obvious and hidden insights. Our modest expertise lies in discerning patterns between and among our respondents' voices, texts and sketches, and in amplifying them so they can be heard and so they can inform our understanding of the role of positive deviance in child protection efforts.

Key Attributes of the Positive Deviance Approach

The following themes and patterns emerged repeatedly in the voices, texts, and sketches of those involved in implementing PD in Uganda and Indonesia. The sub-headings, and the quotations therein, are self-explanatory. Hence, little or no additional explanation is deemed necessary, or provided.

---

53 These totaled some 320 handwritten pages.

The Solutions Lie in Front of our Eyes

In Village Kedoyo, Indonesia, a kader member drew the sketch of a hoe and explained,

> The PD approach is about digging with a hoe. One has to dig to unearth the soil, rocks and nutrients. One needs to turn the soil over to see what lies hidden and buried beneath. Digging brings the fertility of the soil to the surface. Once that is done, even though the soil remains the same, one can plant new crops.

PD is like a hoe....

Paska Aber, the PD project coordinator in Pader District, echoed a similar sentiment with eloquence: "The PD approach encourages the vulnerable to scan their environment and to appreciate the existing community capacities by identifying the present and preferred affordable, sustainable solutions to the community problems."

In Village Gadungsari, Indonesia, a village *kader* who has been involved in the PD program since its inception in 2003, drew a flashlight and explained, "PD is like a flashlight. It helps to shine light and illuminate what hides behind the darkness. It helps us discover what already exists. For example, it helps us discover the existing strengths we had not realized or utilized."

Community Ownership

Raymond,[54] a community leader in Pader District explained: "The PD approach encourages the community to find solutions to their problems from within themselves and this brings satisfaction and fulfilment, which is a much desired value for sustainability." Beatrice,[55] who helped us in implementing our field research in Uganda, agreed:

The PD approach brings about a sense of ownership to the project beneficiaries so that they are in position to continue even when the implementing agency withdraws. The PD approach involves all relevant categories of people in the affected community—whether vulnerable or empowered. This makes the primary beneficiary feel they are still part of the community and develops sense of belonging.

Bonita Birungi, who oversees the PD Project in Pader District out of Save the Children's Kampala office and Pak Kasmadi in Gadungsari, Indonesia both emphasized the following sentiment: "If one is looking for sustainable and rippling change, there is no better community-centered approach than PD."

Opening Lines of Communication, Building Trust

A *kader* in Village Kedoyo, Indonesia, noted, "PD is not about the village chief or the outside change agent imposing what they believe needs to be done. PD is about dialogue and discovery. One learns from seeing first hand what a neighbor does...often by

---

54 Raymond was trained by Jerry Sternin in the PD methodology and also helped us in implementing the present research project.
55 Beatrice, a field worker for CARITAS (a Catholic relief and service organization) in Pader District, was also trained by Jerry Sternin in the PD methodology.

looking over a neighbor's hedge. Then one tries it in one's garden."

PD is about dialogue and self-discovery

A *kader* in Village Kedoyo, Indonesia noted, "People from neighboring villages ask us how their young boys and girls may join our vocational programs. Or how their village could offer equivalence certificates for junior and senior secondary school. They feel that if we can do it, they can do it too."

Simon, a member of the PD implementing team in Pader District, emphasized, "The discovery in PD happens by opening lines of communication. This happens when conversations begin to occur between parties who previously have not communicated openly. PD involves relationship-building and trust."

The PD interventions in Uganda and Indonesia pointed to the virtues of building relationships and trust, demonstrating that trust begets more trust, leading to more open lines of communication and, over time, better outcomes. The personal commitment, hard work and persistence of the PD implementing teams in both locations were palpable. It was clear that Titing Martini[56] in Indonesia and Paska Aber in Uganda believed in the PD approach and the mission of protecting vulnerable children, and embodied a learning attitude toward the unfolding PD interventions. The participatory and non-prescriptive nature of the intervention, and the bringing together of multiple stakeholders (including local government officials), demonstrated a seriousness of purpose. The extensive follow-up inputs on the ground helped strengthen personal relationships, building trust and respect, and allowing for open, immediate, and authentic feedback.

Building Further on Trust and Respect

One of the PD girls in Lukole sub-county, Pader District, Uganda drew the following sketch and explained:

When the PD project got under way, I was very skeptical. I wondered what new things they were going to bring to us this time. I did not understand why we did the community mapping exercise. But as we were doing it I started to see that the map helped us to identify and locate other vulnerable child mothers, our peers. The map was drawn with many of us looking over it and parishes and camps were demarcated. We labeled what was where. We worked with mentors, community members and local leaders who collectively mapped who the most vulnerable girls in the community were, where they lived and how they could be reached.

---

56 At the time this monograph was written, Titing Martini was no longer employed by Save the Children. However, we had the opportunity to obtain her feedback via a teleconference.

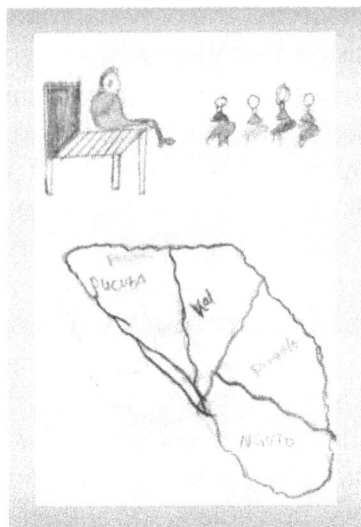

Mapping and meetings:
building trust

The PD girl continued [pointing to the stick figures above the map]:

After the mapping was done, I thought we were done. But we had more meetings...many more. Meetings were held between us and our mentors, between our peer-group members, and with sub-county officials. I've drawn Paska [Save the Children's PD coordinator in Pader District] sitting on the chair—she had a meeting with us and oriented us in this project. She and her team supported us in developing livelihoods and income-generating activities. Slowly, I began to trust that these people were genuinely interested in listening to us, and cared about us.

A member of the PD implementing team in Pader District drew the following two images to talk about how the PD approach builds trust among the beneficiaries by being respectful of their culture. He noted, "In the first sketch, we see the girls singing and dancing their traditional courtship dance. In the PD program, they used this dance as therapy to build self-esteem among the vulnerable girls. That worked very well."

Building trust through local dance forms

He continued:

In the second sketch, you see aunts who served as mentors to the girls, working closely with local county leaders shown with briefcase. Appropriating this aunt-like figure in the Acholi culture as mentors was strategic because they are trustworthy, honest and hardworking. They feel they are responsible and accountable both to the girls and to the county officials. Mentoring through these aunts also meant that the project could be constantly and informally monitored.

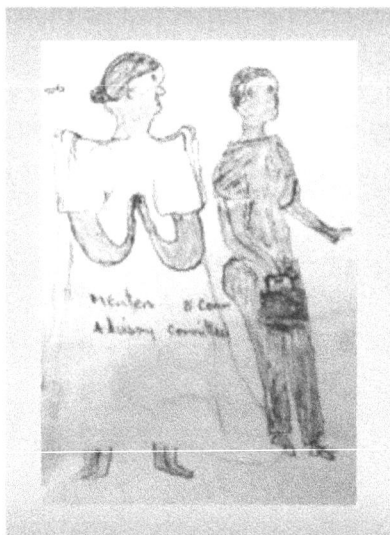

Mentors with county officials: trustworthy links

Another member of the PD implementing team in Uganda echoed the previous sentiment:

> The choice and role of aunt-like mentors—people very accepted by the community as capable of supporting the girls—bridges the gap for girls who do not have parental care and need it. Given they are trustworthy, the counseling and support provided by the mentors and the therapy games and dances they organize builds team spirit, also attracting other girls and families outside the program to take part.

Titing Martini and Bonita Birungi, both of whom provided leadership to the PD projects on child protection in Indonesia and Uganda, respectively, emphasized in personal interviews. Said Martini:

> PD is all about building trust between and among the implementers and the beneficiaries. They have

to recognize that this is not a "hit and run" intervention. So, when working in Gadungsari, our credo was to not hide any information from the community that we may have discerned in the mapping. That built trust and that was a foundation that we could build on.

No Special Resources Needed. Begin Now.

Yuda and Sinta, two kader members in Desa Gadungsari, Indonesia, who had been involved with the PD project from the beginning, drew the following sketch and explained:

PD involves the community identifying a person who is able to solve problems with no extra resources. That is called a PD person. Then the PD methodology tries to identify actionable strategies from the identified behaviors of this person. After a strategy is found, it can be imitated by others right away. The PD approach is thus immediately actionable.

Once PD behaviors are identified,
the approach is immediately actionable

Jimmy, a member of the PD implementing team in Pader District, emphasized, "The use of PD girls as benchmarks who survive in the same environment through no special means encourages and makes it clear to others that the deviant way is possible. There is living proof and now the solution is not abstract. It can be put into use immediately."

In summary, our slate of PD project implementers in both Uganda and Indonesia collectively identified and echoed the following attributes of the PD approach: The solutions lie with the community and are unearthed through self-discovery; the project has sustainability because the community owns the problem and its solution; PD works through the mechanism of social proof; PD thrives on trusting relationships between implementing agency representatives and beneficiaries; and PD is actionable without ado once the PD behaviors are identified by the community.

Lessons Learned about PD as a Child Protection Strategy

What lessons did we learn about PD as a community-centered approach to social change, including its relevance and usefulness for child protection issues, and implications for scalability? Here again, we privilege the voices, texts and sketches of our field-based informants involved in the community of PD practice, without much elaboration, unless necessary.

Lesson #1: The PD Approach to Child Protection is Effective but not Formulaic

The PD approach can be effective in addressing

child protection issues because it privileges local wisdom and resources, providing skills, tools and processes that can be implemented immediately and be sustained over a long period of time. It works as a development approach within a larger context and is not an all-encompassing solution for the prevention of sexual exploitation or realization of child protection. It, however, supplements and complements other efforts—political, humanitarian and activist-centered.

Bonita Birungi, who oversees the PD pilot project in Pader District from Save the Children's Kampala headquarters, explained:

Child protection is defined very differently by different communities. Fundamentally, I believe, that all parents want their children to survive and thrive. In their cultural framework, even if they punish a child, they believe, for the most part, they are doing it because it is better for the child in the long run. This does not mean that punishment is always well-intentioned and we should never intervene. We should. But instead of intervening blindly and without understanding the cultural context, we should try to understand it carefully. Why? Because often pre-prescribed child protection solutions are a-contextual.

Bonita continued:

Take trafficking or engaging in transactional sex as strategies to survive. These may be the well-known ways in which most vulnerable girls or families survive. However, we rarely look at families who have found better ways of surviving. In each community, people have found mechanisms to do it, if only we do not close our eyes to it. We look for outside solutions. What we need to do is to first suspend our prescriptions.

Pak Kasmadi, the PD champion and village secretary in Gadungsari, echoed that sentiment:

PD is not a formula that can be applied anywhere. Even communities that send their girls to work in sex industries may have different reasons. PD is about following certain principles and processes. PD is humble in its approach. It is not about telling; it is about seeing, listening and then bringing the best in the culture forward.

Even though both the PD projects we studied in Uganda and Indonesia deal broadly with "child protection" issues, there are important contextual and topical differences, operating within a cover of overarching similarities. In Uganda, for instance, the PD project is based in a conflict setting and focuses on reintegrating vulnerable child mothers in a community where traditional family structures have broken down, while addressing psychosocial issues faced by former abductees who lived in captivity for many years and were raped, brutalized, and victimized. In contrast, in Indonesia, the PD project is based in a stable, non-conflict area, where the protection issue is to prevent unlawful, unsafe and harmful migration of young girls, and where family and parental structures are largely intact although, as a result of economic gain, perhaps in "silent collusion." In both cases, however, young girls are at risk of unsafe work, sexual exploitation and social marginalization, and the child protection concerns are quite similar.

Although the PD approach to child protection may not be formulaic,[57] that is not to say that there is little or no transfer of learning from pilot to follow-on projects. For instance, Catherine Chen, child protection advisor in Save the Children's Jakarta office, emphasized:

> The Oak Foundation-funded pilot projects in Gadungsari and other East Java communities between 2004 and 2006 were very helpful on at least two counts: the pilot projects provided us with an understanding of proxy indicators of sending and at-risk villages (in terms of migration, unemployment, school drop-out and poverty rates), metrics that were used in conceptualizing the ENABLE project funded by the U.S. Department of Labor. Also, the Oak-funded pilot projects encouraged Save the Children to look at not just having a single-sector PD program (such as in child protection) but a cross-sectoral programmatic approach, given that child protection intersects with education, livelihoods, rights, health, and nutrition.

Lesson #2: The PD Approach Works Best with Real and Intractable Problems

The Indonesian experience with ENABLE allowed for two distinct intervention approaches to girl trafficking—the PD approach in 22 communities and the ENACT approach in 78 communities—and provides some insights into how the severity of the protection

---

57 Although PD-driven child protection responses are influenced by context and topic, the Uganda and Indonesia projects point to a common set of PD strategies that protect children in the longer term by addressing the root causes of problems: family care and support; opportunities for formal and non-formal education; access to capital, business skills training, investing, and savings; mentoring and oversight; peer support groups and social networks; forums for dialogue, discussion, and discovery; and avenues for team-building, discipline, and play.

problem may influence the characteristics of the intervention. As Kirik, member of the PD implementing team based in Surabaya, emphasized:

> Our work in Indonesia suggests that the PD approach may be more useful in villages that have high migration rates coupled with high unemployment, school drop-out and poverty rates: the ones that are the traditional "sending" villages. Here, it makes sense to conduct a PD inquiry and identify PD practices of those families that have not sent their daughters. However, in villages that are at risk—which are not sending areas yet and have low migration rates but high rates of unemployment, school drop-out and poverty—perhaps a community-centered participatory rural appraisal approach with a focus on formal and non-formal education (as in ENACT) may be sufficient.

Although our primary data-collection activities in Indonesia were both based in communities (Gadungsari and Kedoyo) that received the PD intervention, and we did not visit one of the 78 communities that received the ENACT intervention, Kirik's statement deserves attention. What Kirik seems to be saying, drawing upon his intimate field-based knowledge of both the PD and the ENACT interventions, is that the needs and problems in at-risk areas can be sufficiently addressed by using the ENACT intervention model. According to Kirik, the PD inquiry process takes about six months to complete, whereas the ENACT participatory rural appraisal model, which also involved community mapping and mobilization, took only two months in comparison. While PD privileged self-discovery and self-determination and catalyzed motivation to act because of social proof (seeing that someone else within one's surroundings was doing it with the same resources), ENACT combined self-discovery with needs-based programming, gaining some efficiencies while diluting ownership of solutions. Said differently, in a PD intervention, solutions emerge when people begin to understand replicable aspects of existing solutions, rather than working in a prescribed way to solve a problem.

When we probed Kirik and the PD implementing team on this point, they emphasized that PD may not be a required investment in at-risk areas, especially as the problem to be averted—unsafe migration—is not yet a real problem. The Indonesia experience with the application of PD in sending areas (e.g. in Gadungsari and Kedoyo) seemed to confirm that a PD intervention works best when there is an existing and relatively high-volume problem to be mitigated, and when there are existing solutions to those problems within the community.

From the Uganda experience, we gathered that the PD approach, especially in conflict-ridden contexts, can serve multiple roles. It helps build the capacity of vulnerable populations to earn a sustainable livelihood during a war economy. It empowers communities to foster positive relationships both within and outside of peer groups, creating a space for networked business and social participation. And, it enables partnerships with local government and humanitarian structures so that the PD programmatic intervention does not operate in isolation.

A review of the PD literature and our conversations with PD pioneers Jerry and Monique Sternin about the conduct of these two PD projects on child protection yielded additional insights about the conditions under which the PD approach works well: when (1) the solution to the problem is essentially a non-technical one dealing with adaptive behavioral issues, (2) the problem is pervasive and intractable and worth the risk of attempting a new approach, (3) positive deviants do exist within the community, and (4) the community leaders and skilled facilitators are willing to champion the effort, and learning and have faith in the innate wisdom that lies within the community.

Lesson #3: The PD Approach Protects and Prevents

Further, the PD approach interfaces well with core protection issues.[58] It does so by allowing beneficiaries to fully participate in their own protection and, in so doing, empowering them to help protect and support their siblings, family members, and peers.

In both Indonesia and Uganda, young people were involved in the design, implementation, refinement and ongoing assessment of the PD approach. For instance, in Northern Uganda, young girls were involved in the design of the project, beginning with the community mapping activities. They were engaged in peer-to-peer discussions about challenges they face and factors leading to their engagement in transactional sex as well as possible solutions. These girls were consulted and made decisions on the nature of activities and identification of appropriate income-generating activities. These PD girls were looked upon as role models as they supported their siblings, parents and neighbors. By keeping beneficiary participation at the center of the

---

[58] We thank Dan Rono for clarifying our thinking on the interface between PD and child protection.

intervention, PD instills a sense of ownership toward the problems and its solutions.

Further, the PD approach not only can protect "suffering" children from neglect, exploitation and/or violence, it can also serve as prevention programming by empowering the vulnerable children. Usually, it is difficult to address protection and prevention at the same time, yet PD can help out at both ends.

Although PD-driven child protection responses are influenced by context and topic, the Uganda and Indonesia projects point to a common set of PD strategies that protect children in the longer term by addressing the root causes of problems:[59] family care and support; opportunities for formal and non-formal education; access to capital, business skills training, investing and savings; mentoring and oversight; peer-support groups and social networks; forums for dialogue, discussion and discovery; and avenues for team-building, discipline and play.

Lesson #4: Small Inputs, Big impact

Peter Nkhonjera and Bonita Birungi, who provided leadership and oversight to the PD pilot project in Northern Uganda, summarized their perceptions of the project as follows, "Small inputs led to big impact." Peter emphasized, "The change in the girls is palpable. Actually, one can even say unbelievable."

Luc Vanhoorickx, who was involved in the quantitative assessment of the pilot project in Uganda, noted:

---

59 Provided by Dan Rono, Child Protection Advisor, Save the Children. Paraphrased from *Child Protection in Emergencies: Priorities, Principles, Practices.* Sweden: The International Save the Children Alliance, 2007. These terms are also appropriate for non-emergency situations.

The PD project provided far more bang for the dollar compared to what, for instance, food aid does. Small loans of $40 to $50 for the vulnerable girls have led to high levels of empowerment and even savings." Tom Cole, a colleague of Peter, Bonita and Luc added, "In a dominant culture of donor assistance and client dependency, the PD project in Pader seems to be a breath of fresh air. It is amazing that with so little, one can achieve so much."

It was also clear that like other social change approaches, PD can also engender unintended impacts. For instance, in Indonesia, when traffickers (or "brokers") are deprived of a major source of income in one community, they search for others. They also become more creative in their recruiting approaches. We heard of some cases where they lured girls by offering them scholarships and/or convinced their parents by furnishing false "legal" documents. Further, PD's core processes, such as community mapping, laid the groundwork for addressing other social concerns including reproductive health, gender and child rights, and HIV/AIDS.

In Northern Uganda, the need to reduce gender violence emerged as an unintended byproduct of the effectiveness of the PD program. Often, traditional gender roles are displaced by the context of war itself. For instance, young girls who participate in the post-conflict PD program in Uganda sell goods at the market, purchase animals and bicycles, and open a savings account—activities that are traditionally carried out by men. Further, PD girls seek out other people to help them care for their children. Their visible signs of strength and prosperity generate envy and, in some cases, anger. Some community members voiced their concerns about the potential for violent acts against the girls who visibly engage in non-traditional roles.

Lesson #5: Takes Time, Produces Results

A clear pattern echoing among the PD project implementers in both Uganda and Indonesia was: "PD is a very time and skill intensive approach. But, if one is patient, it produces long-lasting and sustainable effects."

As Bonita Birungi noted, "The cost and time of a PD project will vary depending on the scale of the project, the spread of the geographical area, whether or not the context is development or conflict-situated, and what the nature and magnitude of issues to be addressed is.

Robert Omaro, the District Manager of Save the Children's Pader office, emphasized:

> PD has a certain flow to it. When it gets going as it did in Pader, the girls seem to be swimming in a sea of activity, one feeding the other. They do dance, and then they go for debate, and then they go to school, then to the garden, and on and on. They feel that they are *timo mapat* (doing something unique) with the aim of being *lanyut maber* (aspiring to be a PD). In other words, the PD approach has a positive virtuous cycle, it seems.

The pace of implementing a PD project is also a function of the degree of community readiness. While addressing community-centered resistances take time, PD implementers in both Uganda and Indonesia believed that the impact achieved is more than commensurate with the time and resources spent. Local leaders and community members who become proficient in the PD approach continue to use their skills to sustain and strengthen the project, and to apply the approach in other spheres of development.

A *kader* member in village Kedoyo, Indonesia, drew a picture of a lamp and explained: "PD is like a lamp. It guides people. It shows the path. It monitors progress, telling them how much ground has been covered…and how much needs to be done. It restores hope. It burns slowly but surely. One can see there is light at the end of the tunnel."

PD is like a lamp. It burns slowly but surely

Lesson #6: Does not Package Well in a Tool Box

Catherine Chen, child protection adviser in Save the Children's Jakarta office, noted, "As an intervention, PD does not scale well as it is very culture specific. Also, to do PD one needs a competent staff with very specific facilitation skills."

Randa Wilkinson, previously PD nutrition adviser to Save the Children in Jakarta, echoed the sentiment: "PD does not package well in a tool box. Donors want quick results and significant results and want to scale up quickly. However, PD requires mentoring, letting go, putting the community in-charge. That takes time. And, there is no magic wrench."

Lesson #7: Rewriting the Definition of Scalability[60]

Bonita Birungi of Save the Children's Kampala office emphasized:

When we think of scalability of an intervention, we mostly think in terms of geographic scalability: going to an ever widening physical area, reaching more and more people. But that is only one way to think about scaling. How about the scalability that is achieved when an individual who learns about PD processes or PD behaviors applies the learning to another realm of life? For instance, in Uganda, PD for child protection has led to 'food security' for the vulnerable mothers and their children.

---

60 See CORE (2003). Chapter Seven: Expand PD/Hearth Programs. Positive Deviance/Hearth, a resource guide for sustainably rehabilitating malnourished children. Vietnam: Save the Children. Save the Children has extensive experience in scaling up a PD intervention, especially with its nutritional programs in Vietnam. Save the Children Vietnam began in four communities with an approximate total population of 20,000, and it expanded the program to 14 communities with an approximate total population of 80,000. Seven years later, the Vietnam PD/Hearth program reached over 2.2 million people. The CORE PD/Hearth resource guide, which focuses on nutrition programs, includes a five-step process for expansion generated by SC Vietnam. The five steps are: (1) Develop a Small Successful Model—pilot project, (2) Work Out an Expanded Successful Model—streamline for replication while maintaining key elements such as PD Inquiry, (3) Expand the PD/Hearth Approach to the District Level—district-level staff should be involved in the first two steps, (4) Create a "Living University" or "Laboratory for Field Learning"—develop a training of trainers curriculum and impart theory and practice by visiting villages/sites and participating in monitoring and PDI, and (5) Support New Graduates to Return to their Home Base and Begin Replication—each team replicates the approach in two to four communities and once the project is validated the graduates themselves work on expansion and training of trainers.

Bonita continued, "How about the ripple effect: an individual who affects a family, a family that affects the community, which in turn affects other communities?"

In essence, what Bonita seemed to be emphasizing is that the PD approach may not have expeditious geographic scalability for a particular topic (e.g., child protection) because of its time-consuming and skill-intensive facilitation, but it can be scaled to a vast array of cross-sectoral topics and have significant "multiplier" effects through existing social networks.

In responding to the issue of scalability, PD experts Jerry and Monique Sternin agreed with Bonita:

PD may be less effective on scale if we talk about geographic scaling (from a village community, to a district, to a region), but scaling may also mean influencing policy, or promoting the emergence of new leadership, unleashing new social networks or building community capacity. For instance, in Indonesia, the PD project for girls trafficking had the unintended consequence of engendering greater compliance with a government legislation on trafficking, which previously was ignored or overlooked. In Pakistan, the PD project intended to reduce newborn mortality and morbidity not only met its goals but transformed the gender relations between husbands and wives, relationships between mother-in-laws and daughter-in-laws, and made the health providers more accountable to the community. These were real social changes that had a lasting effect on preventing newborn mortality and morbidity. So, the PD approach delivers strongly on quality and sustainability of of change and is scalable in a different way than geographical scaling.

A PD parent in village Kedoyo drew the following sketch and explained, "PD is like a flower: tall, dignified, and beautiful and firmly rooted in soil. When people pause and look at closely, they are charmed by its beauty. It also has a sweet smell which spreads quickly."

PD, a beautiful, sweet-smelling flower

Scalability of a PD project can come in other ways, as well. As Titing Martini, the leader of the Oak-funded PD pilot project on girls trafficking in Indonesia, recalled, "Our initial proposal with the Oak Foundation called for Save the Children to work directly with villagers. But, I realized, there was no way there could be sustainability if we did not partner with a local organization. Also, this way, the local NGO, in this case, LPKP could apply the learning from carrying out a PD intervention to other areas of its work." Indeed, Martini believes that one key learning for LPKP staff from the PD pilot in Gadungsari was to have more faith in the potential of community members to self-discover and self-create; that is, a learning to "let go."

An evaluation report of this project noted, "Bringing in LPKP from the start augurs well for the PD program's sustainability and replicability in East Java. Its early involvement enabled LPKP to experience the whole process of program implementation using the PD approach, admittedly a new 'technology' but one they found to be quite effective.[61]

In Uganda, as well, Save the Children works very closely with sub-county and county level officials in Pader District and existing networks of community leaders so that their experiences in PD transfer to other projects and initiatives over time. One of the community leaders drew the following sketch and explained, "It is strength of the project that Save the Children works closely with sub-county officials and community members in implementing the project. When county officials are involved, they begin to see other problems and a more holistic approach emerges for community development."

Scaling PD through local partnerships

60 A Zenaida and V. Chamaco, *Grassroots anti-trafficking initiatives: Mid-term monitoring and evaluation report.* Save the Children (2004). Provided by SC as background information.

In reflecting on our field-based experiences, we wondered what approach might one take to launch a scalable PD program? Should one start small, i.e., at the local level, and then scale to a wider regional level, or might one start up-front on a bigger geographical scale?

While not an either/or dichotomy, our experiences in Uganda and Indonesia seem to suggest that because of PD's emphasis on amplifying local solutions, principally it makes sense for the PD discovery process to begin at a local level.   On a practical level, starting small also makes sense because while child exploitation can have local, district, regional or national drivers, the effects converge at level of the community, family or an individual.

Planning for expansion entails effective staff recruitment, engendering community engagement and commitment, and the involvement of local NGOs and government officials at local, district and regional levels for pilot reinforcement and sustainability. With key project elements in place, and with some overarching cultural homogeneity in the region of expansion, PD projects can be scaled more rapidly than the pilots. In essence, PD can go fast and wide by beginning slow and small.

In summary, we learned that

PD as a community-centered approach to child protection is influenced deeply by context and topic;
and while PD is not formulaic, it does help with both protection and prevention;
for relatively small inputs PD can yield big

impacts;

PD is time–and skills-intensive but delivers results;

PD does not package well in a toolbox; and

PD is not so easily scalable to cover big populations but can scale along existing social networks and through permanent local stakeholder partnerships.

Recommendations for Building on Investments in Using the Positive Deviance Approach to Protect Children

We provide certain recommendations about harnessing and strengthening the investments in pioneering the PD approach for child protection described in this monograph.

Recommendation #1. The PD Approach Needs Support Over a Longer Term

Unlike other expert-driven social change approaches where problems and solutions are known up front, the PD approach involves a long process of self-discovery and community engagement. For sponsors and donors this means budgeting for a longer initial commitment. For issues as sensitive and complex as child protection issues, project funding commitments should be for at least three years or more, with interim process-oriented deliverables. Programs on such difficult topics require ongoing dialogue with all members of the communities, the demonstration of "social proof" (i.e., the solution to the problem lies locally with a peer), and therefore require time and resources to demonstrate sustainable results.

Recommendation #2. The PD Approach should Be Scaled-Up as a Megacommunity

Barbara Waugh, global personnel director for Hewlett Packard, a self-professed practitioner of the PD approach within HP, and a member of the advisory board of the Positive Deviance Institute at Tufts (constituted by Jerry and Monique Sternin), uses the concept of the *megacommunity* to describe effective programmatic scaling.[62] Waugh advocates scaling a program until it becomes a megacommunity and then repeating the effort in other locales, constantly cross-referencing all efforts across countries for local and broader scale integration and impact.

Waugh defines a megacommunity as a large, ongoing initiative among organizations that share a complex problem, the resolution of which defies unilateral solutions and depends instead on collaboration and a mutual goal. The megacommunity grows through informal networks of people with commitments that they act on together to make a difference. Organizational charters, structures and hierarchies matter much less than people's commitments. Personal relationships are the sinew, conversations represent the blood, and informal networks represent the bones of the communities out of which comprehensive, multiyear, sustainable work arises.

The concept of megacommunities allows us to view PD's global application as part of an evolving network, not as an isolated event. There is value in creating clusters of PD networks by region, and PD megacommunities that spill beyond regional and national borders. We see this in the case of PD/Hearth in

62 Waugh, B. (2007). HP engineers as a megacommunity. *The Megacommunity Way.* Kleiner A. & Delurey, M., eds. strategy + business books.

Vietnam where many trainees go through the reflective and problem-posing methodology together through the Living University in Quang Xuong. Similarly, the newly instituted PD resource center at the University of Indonesia can become the locus of another cluster of PD learners and trainers. And as these clusters are networked, we begin to see that learners and trainers can be "recycled," so the initial monetary and human investment is always producing, i.e., paying dividends. The financial and human investment can yield sustained social impact at the local PD site because it is supported on a global level.

Recommendation #3. PD projects need greater emphasis on monitoring and evaluation

All PD projects should have strong monitoring and evaluation components, utilizing a wide variety of quantitative and qualitative methodologies acting in concert. The past documentation of PD projects, including the present one, was uneven between and across methodologies and the two sites. More careful attention to incorporating monitoring and evaluation processes from the inception of the project will allow PD sponsors and users to codify their intellectual capital and disseminate it both within and outside.

Here it is important to emphasize that PD projects, on account of their community-driven, process-oriented nature, can greatly benefit from incorporating participatory sketching and narration activities (as was employed in the present study). Such methods allow, at very low cost, for participants to express themselves in ways that are not possible in surveys, providing a richer understanding of their struggles, triumphs and failures, and the social mechanisms which influence those outcomes.

Our research in Uganda and Indonesia generated an array of rich visual and textual data that holds important implications for attending to, and proactively developing, culturally relevant, user-defined metrics of assessment and measurement. Often textbook–derived empowerment scales are highly (1) textual, that is, reading a line of text and asking whether a respondent agrees or disagrees, and (2) a-contextual, that is, framed in the researcher's academic worldview and not embedded in participants' contexts of understanding. In Uganda, for instance, the sketches depicting clotheslines, which may go unnoticed under ordinary circumstances, represent a rich multitextured measure of (1) personal hygiene (washing clothes), (2) quality of life (number of clothes on the line), (3) social status in the community, and (4) personal worth. In the respondents' worldview, these artifacts may have deeper significance and meaning than a researcher may be able to grasp. Another example is the depiction of a mat in front of an Acholi house in dozens of sketches, which signifies that one is at peace with oneself, is available to welcome and greet others, and is open to engage in a conversation. The mat under a tree is thus a culturally robust measure of one's psychosocial status, as well as an indicator of a person's social networking patterns.

Attention to, and understanding of, such culturally embedded measures is a first step in designing people-centered evaluation systems. Such a mindset is also completely consistent with the philosophical basis of the positive deviance approach.

References

Aber, P. 2007. *Baseline Survey for Save the Children, U.S. on Formerly Abducted Girl Mothers and other Vulnerable Girls, Pader District, Northern Uganda*. Save the Children Federation, Inc.

---. 2007. Piloting the Positive Deviance Approach in Child Protection Intervention

---.2007. Report on community mapping exercise.

---.2007. Report on PDI rapid assessment.

Annan. J, Blattman C., Carlson, K., Mazurana, D. 2008. The state of female youth in Northern Uganda: Findings from the survey of war affected youth (SWAY). The Feinstein International Center. Available at https://wikis.uit.tufts.edu/confluence/display/FIC/The +State+of+Female+Youth+in+Northern+Uganda-- Findings+from+the+Survey+of+War+Affected+Youth

Berkeley-Tulane Initiative on Vulnerable Populations. 2007. Abducted: The Lord's Resistance Army and forced conscription in northern Uganda. Available at http://www.reliefweb.int/rw/RWB.NSF/db900SID/EVO D-76JJG5?OpenDocument

Bouta, T. & Frerks, G. 2002. *Women's roles in conflict prevention, conflict resolution, and post-conflict reconstruction*. Netherlands Institute of International Relations.

Bertels T., Sternin J. 2003. *Rath and Strong's Six Sigma Leadership Handbook*. Hoboken, NJ: John Wiley and son's Inc. p. 450-457.

Buscell, P. 2004. The power of positive deviance. *Emerging*, The Newsletter of the Plexus Institute August-October, 8-20.

Cilliers, J. 2004. Evidence and analysis: Post-conflict reconstruction in Africa: Breaking the conflict trap through development. Paper prepared for the Commission for Africa.

CORE. 2003. Chapter Seven: Expand PD/Hearth Programs. *Positive Deviance/Hearth*, a resource guide for sustainably rehabilitating malnourished children. Vietnam: Save the Children.

Dorsey, D. 2000. Positive deviant. *Fast Company*, 41, 284-292.

Internal Displacement Monitoring Centre (IDMC). 2008. Uganda: Uncertain future for IDPs while peace remains elusive. Available at www.internal-displacement.org

IRIN 2008. Uganda: Optimism prevails despite setback in peace talks.
http://www.irinnews.org/report.aspx?ReportId=77823

Macklis, R.M. 2001. Successful patient safety initiatives: Driven from within. *Group Practice Journal*, 50(10), 1-5.

Martini, T. 2005. PD for girl trafficking prevention: Experience from south Malang. *PD Bulletin* Vol. 1 No. 4. http://www.positivedeviance.org/materials/publications.html

Nutrition Working Group, Child Survival Collaborations

and Resources Group (CORE). 2002. *Positive Deviance / Hearth: A Resource Guide for Sustainably Rehabilitating Malnourished Children*, Washington, D.C.

LPKP Jawa Timur, Save the Children Indonesia. The Positive Deviance Approach for preventing girl trafficking.
http://www.positivedeviance.org/projects/indgirltraffi ck/

Pascale, R.T., and Sternin, J. 2005. Your company's secret change agents. *Harvard Business Review*. May, 1-11.

Pascale, R.T., Millemann, M., & Gioja2000. *Surfing the edge of chaos: The laws of nature and the new laws of business.* New York: Crown Publishing Group.

Positive Deviance Initiative/Save the Children in Indonesia. 2005. Two years after the workshop - Gadung Sari village.
http://www.positivedeviance.org/projects/indgirltraffi ck/updateApr2006.html.

The International Save the Children Alliance.2007. Child Protection in Emergencies: Priorities, Principles, and Practices. Sweden: The International Save the Children Alliance.

Save the Children—IFO.2005. *Brief information on Save the Children-IFO trafficking prevention program*. Save the Children Federation, Inc. Provided by SC as background information.

Save the Children. 2006. Final project document under USDOL and Save the Children, Inc. cooperative agreement.   Washington D.C.: Save the Children

Federation, Inc.

Singhal, A., and Devi, K. 2003. Visual Voices in Participatory Communication. Communicator, 37, 1-15.

Singhal, A. and Greiner, K. 2007. "Do What you Can, With What you Have, Where you Are": A Quest to Eliminate MRSA at the Veterans Health Administration's hospitals in Pittsburgh. *Deep Learning*, Volume 1(4), pp. 1-14. Complexity-in-Action Series. Allentown, NJ: Plexus Institute.

Singhal, A., and Rattine-Flaherty, E. 2006. Pencils and Photos as Tools of Communicative Research and Praxis: Analyzing Minga Perú's Quest for Social Justice in the Amazon. *Gazette*, 68(4), 313-330.

Sparks, D. 2004. From hunger aid to school reform: An interview with Jerry Sternin. Journal of Staff Development, 25(1), 12-21.

Sternin, J. 2003. *Practice positive deviance for extraordinary social and organizational change.* In D. Ulrich, M. Goldsmith, L. Carter, J. Bolt, and N. Smallwood (eds.), The change champion's fieldguide (pp. 20-37). New York: Best Practice Publications.

Sternin, J. 2003. Transcription of workshop/meeting with LPKP staff and village kaders. The full transcription of the 3 hour and 45 minute session is available on the Positive Deviance webpage:
http://www.positivedeviance.org/projects/indgirltraffi ck/kaders_workshop.pdf

Sternin J. and Choo R. (2000). The Power of Positive Deviance. *Harvard Business Review*, January-February

2000: 14-15.

Sternin, M., Sternin, J. and Marsh, D. 1999. Scaling up poverty alleviation and nutrition program in Vietnam. In T. Marchione (ed.), *Scaling up, scaling down* (pp. 97-117). Gordon and Breach Publishers.

UNICEF 2008. *UNICEF Humanitarian Action update: Uganda*, April 25, 2008. Available at http://www.unicef.org/infobycountry/files/Uganda_H AU_Apr08.pdf

Vanhoorickx, L., Aber, P., Odong, S.L.2008. *Positive deviance with vulnerable girls—first year assessment report*. Save the Children in Uganda.

Waugh, B. 2007. HP engineers as a megacommunity. *The Megacommunity Way*. Kleiner A. & Delurey, M., eds. strategy and business books.

WebPD Intro.2005. Materials/Bibliography: Presentations. www.positivedeviance.org

Zenaida, A., Chamaco, V. 2004. Grassroots anti-trafficking initiatives: Mid-term monitoring and evaluation report. Save the Children Federation, Inc.

Zeitlin, M., Ghassemi, H., and Mansour, M. 1990. *Positive deviance in child nutrition*. New York: UN University Press.